P9-CPW-118

More Praise for *The Gender Intelligent Retailer*

"When a woman walks into your store, she's likely already packed the kids' lunches, negotiated the need for socks with a crying toddler, organized dinner, and had a client breakfast . . . all before 10! If you don't make her experience as positive as possible and treat her with respect, she'll tell all her friends where not to shop. Find out the keys to success in Joanne and Sean's comprehensive, witty, and practical guide. And here's the good news: if you build it, they will come, women and men."

Anne Kothawala, President, Canadian Newspaper Association

"Through an engaging collection of facts and stories woven together with sharp wit and humor, Joanne Thomas Yaccato provides practical guidance to awaken business leaders to a significant opportunity available in today's marketplace. *The Gender Intelligent Retailer* brings to life a critical insight: transitioning to an organization that takes a holistic view inclusive of women consumers is not something you do, it is something you become."

Kevin Regan, Executive Vice President, Investors Group

"Most business books use a 'marketing to women' lens when advising companies on the hows and wherefores of reaching women consumers. *The Gender Intelligent Retailer* makes quick work of that approach and nails the *real* business case for understanding women consumers. Using her concept of Gender Intelligence intertwined in a wonderful blend of case studies, hilarious personal anecdotes, hard-core research and 'news you can use,' Joanne Thomas Yaccato reveals that the real pay off for companies is simply this—make something women friendly, you make it everybody-friendly."

Amanda Ellis, Lead Specialist, Gender and Development, The World Bank Group

"*The Gender Intelligent Retailer* provides theory and practicum—what works and doesn't work—and quantifies it. Thomas Yaccato and McSweeney nudge you outside your comfort zone with a holistic 'gender conscious' retail approach that promises to build a loyal shopping base and keep you ahead of the pack."

Bob Kowynia, Manager, North American Advertising & Communications, Lennox Industries

"For those hoping to succeed in the coming decades, this book offers great insight into the influence with which gender-sensitive initiatives benefit the retail realm. It demonstrates how advantageous a female-friendly approach is to any contemporary business model and its subsequent bottom line. A must read!"

Rossana Di Zio Magnotta, Chief Executive Officer and President, Magnotta Winery Corporation

"As a marketing researcher, I am regularly asked to profile consumers to help companies create more audience-focused marketing strategies. One of the first things retailers might examine is the differences between men and women. The challenge is that these segments are so easy to identify but so difficult to understand. Joanne's insights provide marketers and business leaders with the path to the big picture conversations and honest reflections that researchers would like to contribute to more often. She inspires the necessary shift from a simple focus on gender targets to a whole new way of thinking that may enable powerful growth and expansion for retailers and consumer-facing business."

Robert Daniel, President, Maritz Research Canada

The Gender Intelligent Retailer

The Gender Intelligent Retailer

Discover the Connection Between Women Consumers and Business Growth

Joanne Thomas Yaccato with Sean McSweeney

John Wiley & Sons Canada, Ltd.

Copyright © 2008 by Joanne Thomas Yaccato and Sean McSweeney

All rights reserved. No part of this work covered by the copyright herein may be reproduced or used in any form or by any means—graphic, electronic or mechanical without the prior written permission of the publisher. Any request for photocopying, recording, taping or information storage and retrieval systems of any part of this book shall be directed in writing to The Canadian Copyright Licensing Agency (Access Copyright). For an Access Copyright license, visit www.accesscopyright.ca or call toll free 1-800-893-5777.

Care has been taken to trace ownership of copyright material contained in this book. The publisher will gladly receive any information that will enable them to rectify any reference or credit line in subsequent editions.

Library and Archives Canada Cataloguing in Publication Data

Thomas Yaccato, Joanne, 1957–
   The Gender Intelligent Retailer / Joanne
Thomas Yaccato, Sean McSweeney.

Includes bibliographical references and index.
ISBN 978-0-470-84102-0

   1. Women consumers. 2. Target marketing. 3. Marketing—Psychological aspects. 4. Selling—Psychological aspects. I. McSweeney, Sean, 1968– II. Title.

HC79.C6T486 2008   658.8'04   C2008-902162-2

Production Credits
Cover design: Ian Koo
Cover image: ©istockphoto.com/Kirsty Pargeter
Interior text design: Ian koo
Typesetting: Thomson Digital
Printer: Friesens

John Wiley & Sons Canada, Ltd.
6045 Freemont Blvd.
Mississauga, Ontario
L5R 4J3

This book is printed with biodegradable vegetable-based inks on 60lb. recycled white paper, 100% post-consumer waste.

Printed in Canada

1 2 3 4 5 FP 11 10 09 08

To our children; Patrick, Connor, Kieran, Maeve and Kathleen (4/5ths of this list is Sean's!), our long suffering and patient spouses, Michael and Nicole and, as always, our biggest fan club—our mothers, Karen Wheeler and Dianne Thomas Yaccato.

To retail managers working in an under-appreciated industry, who try to create value and innovation in a tough, fluid and dynamic business environment . . . and to the women consumers who actively nudge them along.

Table of Contents

Acknowledgements

I'm always amazed where I find ideas and support for book projects, invariably in the oddest of places. Who'd have thought that the very earnest young man I interviewed for *The 80% Minority* five years ago from Mountain Equipment Co-Op would become a crucial member of my company's team, let alone become my talented co-author. Sean's retail expertise, but more importantly, his innate understanding of women consumers never ceases to amaze me. He teaches me every day.

Who would have thought the parent of the new kid in my daughter's class would earn the highly-prized nickname of Helen "Pit Bull" Bullingham because she turned out to be such a committed and amazing (though devastatingly honest) technical adviser right to the very end.

I never dreamed that the new family that moved on our street would be former farmers and that Tim, the dad, held an MBA from Guelph's prestigious Agricultural College. His command of all things "business" and "agricultural" gave this book the necessary glue to beautifully tie together otherwise disparate themes.

And when the inevitable waves of writer's despair came crashing down, that unfailing presence in my computer, David Morash, always gave me the belly laugh I needed to help pull myself up by the proverbial boot straps.

It's always an important boost to the writer's psyche to get strong industry encouragement, which came our way through Rob Daniel, president of Maritz Research and Diane Briseboise, president of The Retail Council of Canada. They both supported this project in a myriad of very important ways and for that, Sean and I will be eternally grateful. The gang at Wiley also deserve special mention. Robert Harris, Jennifer Smith and Karen Milner took a grand total of 13 seconds to see the importance of this book and signed on right away. The writing/editing process was by no means easy. Special nod to Pam Vokey for being such a brilliant listener and being so adept at calming ruffled feathers.

No book ever gets to completion without my right hand and assistant of 15 years, Rosa Morra. It's pretty simple, without Rosa—nothing—let alone a book, gets done. Lucy Tanguay, my very favourite business partner also added her wisdom and unique perspective throughout making *The Gender Intelligent Retailer* a much better book. OK. I'll shut up now. It's Sean's turn.

Sean here. I'd like to acknowledge all of my teachers, coaches and mentors but there is one in particular that needs special mention. During my competitive days as a whitewater athlete, this coach told me to "paddle like a woman" because of my smaller stature. This fundamentally changed the way I thought about the world and led me to where I am today.

I want to thank all my colleagues at Mountain Equipment Co-op, an organization that I consider to be the finest retailer in the world. I have learned a great deal from my customers, co-workers and senior managers and they have significantly influenced my thinking. Thank you Don Serl, who taught me the value of rational, well-thought ideas and to not get distracted by the hype. I have had the good fortune to work for Steven Cross and Bob Matheson, who taught me what it means to be a retail professional.

To my co-author and mentor, Joanne Thomas Yaccato, who, five years ago, somehow managed to see something in me and helped me to "deliver" a book—my greatest professional achievement to date. Even more importantly, she taught me about delivering value and results in the real world of business. I am more grateful than words can express.

We both would like to thank our spouses, family and friends who have spent two years of their lives with this book as their constant companion. My 13-year old daughter Kate has grown up with "author" mom and has been through this process six times. Thankfully, she (along with my very patient husband Michael) has developed a cavalier attitude to mom's bizarre hours and wild writer mood swings. It's become "no-biggy". However, Sean is new to this game. He *in particular* thanks his circle for all for their patience and love during a very steep learning curve, while balancing life as a novice author, father of four (under 9), active athlete and working for a pay cheque at MEC.

Finally, we'd like to thank the women consumers of the world who give Sean and I what we need to get it right. They are patient, intelligent, innovative, humourous and powerful, something every retailer should strive for.

Preface

Most of us live in disconnected "silos." Our lives are compartmentalized into work, play, and family. The business world is divided into internal departments, competition, financial markets, and consumers. We run our lives and our businesses as though they were some kind of giant, metaphorical file folder. Yet, most definitions of success that I've seen, whether in life or in business, have their genesis in everything, operating as a synchronistic whole. However, it's pretty rare to see this kind of integrated synchronicity. While this may seem rather esoteric for a book on retailing, it really isn't. We've led companies to increased market share and customer satisfaction levels by convincing them to think like organic farmers. They don't see land as purely income-producing plots of dirt but as an intrinsic part of a whole, a pretty powerful metaphor for both our personal and business lives.

My company, The Thomas Yaccato Group, is in the silo-busting business. We've been around for more than 15 years, bringing companies together with women consumers. In essence, we are helping to create new corporate "ecosystems." An ecosystem, as defined in a classic sense, is simply an ecological community functioning as a unit together with its environment.

When we've seen things really connect and work as an integrated whole or an ecosystem, when they coexist rather than dominate, we've witnessed astounding results in terms of increased market share and customer satisfaction levels. Starting in 2001, one year into a four-year project during which we trained 2,000 Royal Bank account managers on how to take women entrepreneurs seriously, the company experienced a 10 percent increase in women's market share (in an industry where blood spills to garner a 2 percent increase) and a 29 percent increase in customer satisfaction levels with women entrepreneurs and their account managers.

It's simply about this: Women are incredibly discerning consumers who control 80 percent of the consumer dollar spent in the industrialized world. We have categorically proven over and over again that if you focus on what women want in a retail experience, you raise the bar for *everyone*. Using a gender lens™ when looking at your business is much more than just casually looking at things from a woman's point of view. It's as much about having a wider view of all of the issues that face your business. We've coined a new adage: If you make it women-friendly, you make it everybody-friendly.

The "we" in all of this is the guy on the cover of this book. Sean McSweeney is the brainchild and powerhouse behind the enormously successful shift from unisex to gender-based retailing of Canada's darling retailer, Mountain Equipment Co-op (MEC). I first met Sean when I profiled MEC for *The 80% Minority: Reaching the Real World of Women Consumers*. The Toronto store is one of MEC's flagship stores and is considered one of the greenest retail buildings in North America. MEC not only boasts green roofs, solar power, and the ability to reclaim/recycle 95 percent of operational waste, they also lead by donating 1 percent of revenue to environmental conservation and education projects. Sean himself is a committed bike commuter, rain or shine, and has led the Toronto store to win a number of environmental awards.

Sean knocked my pantyhose off with his practical approach to including women's preferences, perspectives, and world view into everything MEC does. This wasn't revolutionary or rocket science to him. "Bloody common sense," he grumbles. Sean led changes in the Toronto store that have contributed to a rather intriguing demographic shift at MEC. It moved from 70 percent male to 50/50, with women representing the largest area of growth for the company.

So, it turns out that both Sean and I are business people, greenies, feminists, and parents. We buy organic, care about the Earth, diversity, gender inclusion, business cases, bottom lines, and kids. What's interesting though, since turning 50, the dividers separating these somewhat "siloed" parts of my life have been crashing down all around me at an accelerated rate.

I've come to the conclusion that all of life's experiences and perspectives, no matter how divergent or apparently unrelated, have actually been lying about on some metaphysical compost heap. Years of experience in environmental causes, the retail industry, and Gender Intelligence™ have all been fermenting on this compost heap and have now been transformed into a highly productive, rich, harmonized humus or world view. The result is a process we've called Gender-Intelligent Retail Ecology™ or GIRE. The purpose of GIRE is to help companies take stock of their current retail ecosystem and move to one that is more women-centric or organic.

Developing a gender-intelligent retail ecosystem™ is corporate-speak for "going organic"—that is, becoming more women-centric. It's *not* about creating a "marketing-to-women" philosophy, department, or position that is separate and distinct from how business normally gets done. It's a framework that provides companies with a sustainable foundation to *intelligently and authentically* connect with women consumers. Its core, gender intelligence™, ensures that women's world view, preferences, and life realities are incorporated into everything the company does. This, in turn, creates a companywide core competency that ensures that women consumers' needs are actually intrinsic to how business operates, something woefully lacking today.

Pick up any newspaper or magazine and chances are pretty good that someone will be howling at the moon about the dangers of traditional monoculture in farming. We now think a similar phenomenon is beginning to take hold in the retail industry. There is a noticeable trend in companies coming to us, depressed over declining market share. Entrenched short-term attitudes that are pervasive both in retail and agriculture are no longer effective. We've seen and experienced—up close and personal-like—companies achieve impressive short- and long-term results by simply integrating a wide-angle gender lens throughout their organization. This is the heart and soul of developing a gender-intelligent retail ecosystem. This book will tell you how to get started, but, as Sean is quick to point out, "At MEC, our work will never be done. Success is constantly being in the 'getting there' stage."

We have proof that GIRE is an incredibly effective way to create an environment that women want to visit, spend their money in, and tell all of their friends about. So, to get a clearer picture, we invite you to cast off your ties and heels and don your rubber boots and overalls. We're heading to the fresh air of the farm.

CHAPTER ONE

Down on the Farm . . .

The simple principle of life is to find out what she wants and give it to her. It's worked in my marriage for 35 years and it works in laundry.[1]

—A.G. Lafley, CEO, Procter & Gamble

WHY RETAIL IS LIKE FARMING

My neighbour, Tim Smith, was actually a farmer before he became my neighbour. Tim is a real character, with a devilish sense of humour and a wonderfully balanced world view about farming. He explains to us novices that conventional agriculture is about cultivating a space and achieving the best yield possible in that space. It takes advantage of the "economies of scale" principle. However, Tim goes on to point out that, over the last 10 years, farmers have finally realized that monoculture has become a big problem. A monoculture is a single crop that is harvested, processed, and marketed without differentiation.

The Perils of Retail Monoculture

Our guy Sean, a lifelong retail man, maintains that today's retail environment is actually the business equivalent of monoculture. "Retailers tend to broad-brush their consumer base with the same

---

1   Sarah Ellison, "P&G Chief's Turnaround Recipe: Find Out What Women Want," *Wall Street Journal* (June 1, 2005): A1.

brush, with inadequate recognition of diversity. Everyone is sold the same stuff the same way. Those companies that do decide to differentiate women often fall prey to what we call pink-washing, which are strategies that invariably lack depth, substance, variety, or authenticity."

By retail monoculture, we are specifically referring to retail management and a strategic world view that employs only a narrow vision. Monoculture is evident in company head offices where a MAWG (middle-aged white guy) syndrome can flourish. Therefore, the filter used can be pretty one-dimensional. We'll speak about this in Chapter 4, but think beer and car companies, the investment business, and, believe it or not, even certain cosmetics companies. (It's not always the traditional "male bastions.")

While the upside of retail monoculture is clear—economic efficiencies, knowing your market extremely well, etc.—there are very serious downsides to monoculture, whether your product is potatoes or pantyhose.

"Retailers," Sean explains, "exhibit a strong focus on supply chain management and lower prices. This means more and more companies are finding themselves having to constantly 'fertilize' in order to stay relevant. More resources are needed just to keep up current levels of production. Not only does this take a significant toll on a company's ability to stay viable, the strategies generally used to maximize yield almost always fail women consumers. This includes things like the old tried-and-true 'stack 'em high and watch 'em fly' mantra, as well as offering products and services in a good-better-best hierarchy. There is a famous marketing mantra: 'People buy solutions, not products.' Women in particular seek solutions that this good-better-best product hierarchy will not address. It doesn't look at a product lineup holistically and if you see your product only in a hierarchical framework, often you miss the value and solution that it provides."

In a nutshell, it looks like this:

A traditional farmer practising monoculture has a very one-dimensional view of the world (and his or her product), and often operates on the premise of perceived short-term efficiency despite the damage done to the environment and missed opportunities to do things better. Retailers who are traditionalists meet the needs of women consumers through a one-dimensional "marketing-to-women" lens, and concentrate on short-term efficiency, missing out on profits and, in the end, damaging shareholder value.

Almost every North American car company is suffering as the result of this type of short-term thinking and the consumer experience for women continues to be below par, yet Japanese companies are kicking butt. The *Globe and Mail* reported on a study of the relationship between customer satisfaction and stock prices, and found a strong link. The researchers found that between February 18, 1997 and May 21, 2003, a hypothetical portfolio based on American Customer Satisfaction Index (ACSI) data outperformed the Dow Jones Industrial Average by 93 percent and the Standard & Poor's 500-stock index by 201 percent. A second, real-world portfolio also outshone the S&P 500 in each year between 2000 and 2004. Companies that performed well on the stock market were Toyota Motor Corp., Apple Computer Inc., and Google Inc., and were also companies that scored high on the ACSI. Companies like Ford Motor Co. scored at the low end of the scale.

An organic farmer looks at everything holistically; no one element of farming is left out of the cycle. It's also an attitude. A gender-intelligent retailer does the same. Women's consumer needs and preferences are intrinsic to all parts of the planning and strategy cycle, not just in marketing. Gender intelligence is an attitude as well. But in the corporate world, to make things holistic, we first need to break down the pieces by using a gender-based filter and then put the pieces back together again.

It's not that the business model necessarily changes, though it can. In the retail and services world, companies need to develop products and services, conduct market research, market, advertise, and sell their goods and services. This doesn't change when a company creates a gender-intelligent ecosystem. It's just that these areas now have a gender-conscious lens in their approach to doing everything. And believe me, it's badly needed.

In the business world, this critically important gender-lens file folder seems to be stuck in the bottom drawer. Women make most of the consumer buying decisions, but even more compelling is that women consumers, much more so than men, are incredibly attuned to the micro-level detail of the *entire* consumer process. This is a process that starts from a comment made by a friend, the first phone call or the first visit to the company's website, and runs straight through to after-sales customer service and the company's presence in the community. According to our research, women could tell if a company understood their needs by the way a salesperson talked to them. These highly developed consumer antennae can create a great deal of pressure on an unsuspecting company.

INCENTIVE TO MAINTAINING THE STATUS QUO IN RETAIL

Retailers are locked to the status quo. Much of what you see as a consumer at the store level is the result of buying decisions made up to 18 months before and, in some instances, designed and developed two to three years earlier. What lives in the store/office today is often a retailer's or service provider's best guess at what the landscape will look like months to years out. Not surprisingly, they are committed to this inventory or service because they now "own" it.

This can result in an organization becoming resistant to change. Even if you want to change your product, the reality of the global supply chain makes it tough. Suppliers have plenty on the line because they make a sizable investment in building product a certain way. However, Graeme Spicer, a Toronto-based retail strategist with years of experience tucked under his belt working with giants like Wal-Mart and Bata Retail, explains from his perspective that change may be in the wind. "Retailers are waking up to the concept of 'speed to market' resulting in increasingly compressed product development cycles and leaner inventory."

Retailers and service folk have a lot committed in their physical store/office layouts. In a retail store, shelving is expensive. The retail world also has very little downtime to get things done. Any retailer of any significant size is stocking through the night. It's a business that is essentially running 24/7 to meet consumer needs. If you have to make any changes, it's difficult to do so without interrupting the business. This can make the whole enterprise, both management and store employees, cranky because it can have a rather negative effect on revenues.

By no means are we minimizing or dismissing these very real issues. But the fact remains that the traditional retail practice of selling in the same way to everyone without taking into account the diversity of consumers and, in particular, women, who make most of the consumer decisions, simply doesn't work. The conventional marketing-to-women approach flourishes because it doesn't require a major shift in the organization. This business model looks at meeting the needs of women as an "event" or something special to do or create, rather than as an integrated business core competency.

Change is a big deal in any organization, but gender intelligence is as much about a way of thinking about problems and business challenges as it is about radically altering your organization. Most of the companies that we profile in this book took on some big changes, but, equally important, they started to think differently. They have started using a gender lens, something that hugely impacts the future.

In retail, it's pretty important to know how your customers are feeling. In a gender-based study that we conducted with Maritz Research in 2007, we asked 1,000 Canadian women and men their world view about the stars and dogs of the retail and services world. This is what we found:

Well over half of the women in our study said they had experienced a retail situation where *they felt they were being treated less seriously* because of their gender. Almost three times as many women than men made this statement.

But here's the paradox. Seventy-one percent of the women in our study said they were *the key decision maker* regarding consumer purchases in the household, with 42 percent of men saying the same thing.

● Overall, women, much more so than men, report being treated less seriously
  because of their gender.

   ● For women, occurrences of being treated less seriously increased with age
     until 55, at which point reported occurrences decrease.

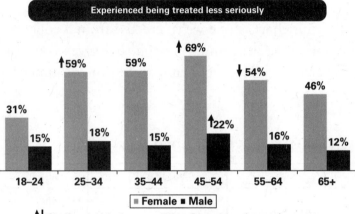

Experienced being treated less seriously

| 18–24 | 25–34 | 35–44 | 45–54 | 55–64 | 65+ |

Female: 31%, ↑59%, 59%, ↑69%, ↓54%, 46%
Male: 15%, 18%, 15%, ↑22%, 16%, 12%

■ Female ■ Male

↑↓ Significantly higher/lower at a 95% confidence interval vs. previous age group

● Retail experiences, good or bad, will be shared by the majority of women.

   ● Women have a very strong influence on purchases made for the household,
     much more so than men.

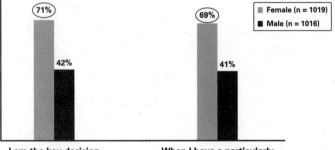

Female (n = 1019)
Male (n = 1016)

71% / 42% — I am the key decision maker around most consumer purchases in the household

69% / 41% — When I have a particularly good or bad retail experience, I tell my friends and family about it

◯ Significantly higher at a 95% confidence interval   Scores shown are Top 2 box on a 5 point scale

Men don't tend to say or do much about bad experiences. Forty-one percent of discontented male consumers tell friends and family about a bad experience. If a woman is ticked off, close to 70 percent go on the verbal warpath.

The following chart is one we've created from a collection of our own and other academic research that gives you some sense of how gender differences can manifest in consumer behaviour.

CONSUMER-BASED GENDER DIFFERENCES

	WOMEN	MEN
What is our decision-making process?	• intuitive • subjective • decisions made after each detail is explored	• rational • objective • straight to the point
What are their dominant decision criteria?	• relationship with customer point of contact • prefer mentor rather than adviser	• the job the salesperson does
How do they view negotiation?	• win-win	• win-lose
How do clients want to be closed?	• suggestive	• directive
How do we gauge performance?	• quality of advice and relationship, not just performance	• performance relative to others
How do we achieve the highest-quality relationships?	• performance plus relationship	• achievement in and of itself

(Continued)

How can we continue to motivate relationships?	• inspiration from within • women want their salesperson and their friends to succeed, therefore more likely to refer	• logic—what can you produce?
How should you deal with problems as they occur?	• want to share, not solve • opportunity to build on the "relationship" dimension	• want them fixed • will still work with you even if the relationship is not ideal
How do we achieve results?	• common ground • rapport	• competition • hierarchy

We've also discovered women are inherently "organic." A statistically significant higher number of women than men said they would change brand to support the environment. Women's organic nature is also why you'll see corporate responsibility and business practices, especially regarding the environment, ranking high on the must-have list with the majority of women consumers. These issues are equally important to men, but our research showed these are *much greater drivers of loyalty for women than they are for men.* Women are more observant of company practices and how well they match with the company's image. Heaven knows we've heard from marketers that people *say* they want this stuff, but when the rubber hits the road, they aren't willing to pay for it. Our experience reveals that it's likely the fault of the company in terms of how the benefits are communicated. Our research revealed that women see marketing and advertising having little relevance to their lives.

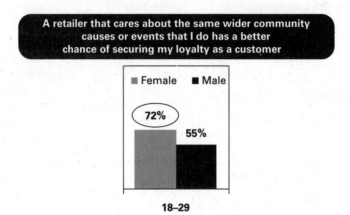

A retailer that cares about the same wider community causes or events that I do has a better chance of securing my loyalty as a customer

Female   Male

72%

55%

18–29

Here's a fascinating twist on the corporate practices issue: US-based Women's Business Enterprise National Council (WBENC) recently did a study that revealed 80 percent of women consumers would be compelled to try a company's product or service if they were not already a customer if they knew a company used women-owned businesses as vendors. Another 80 percent said awareness of a company's practice of buying from women's businesses would moderately or significantly solidify their brand loyalty. And a majority, 51 percent, would even give a company a second chance if the product or service missed the mark the first time.

So, women make most of the consumer decisions; literally line up to shop at companies that support other women, and the local and global community; have a jungle telegraph so comprehensive it should force retailers to their knees purely out of respect—and women consumers feel that they aren't treated seriously? As my 12-year-old says, "What's up with that?!" If believing that they are not being taken as seriously as men is the genesis of women consumers' discontent with the status quo, then the status quo better give its head a collective shake. It's pretty clear that companies need to adopt an entirely different business perspective than the one in vogue at the moment. And what is in vogue is that whole "marketing-to-women" premise—something separate and distinct from how business usually gets done.

Women, being astute consumers, can smell a "femmarketing" rat a mile away, which leads us to the basic premise of this book: Not only do companies need to expand their perspective to be more inclusive of women consumers' needs, they need to do so in a way that takes them seriously. And if they do so in a way that takes women seriously, all consumers benefit. Big time.

IT IS *NOT* ABOUT "MARKETING-TO-WOMEN"

Let me assure you, dear readers, that there isn't some kind of Mike Myers–inspired Dr. Evil character heading up a clandestine international conspiracy with the sole mandate of pissing off women. It's worse than that. There are millions of characters running companies who don't even acknowledge or see women at all. Or (shudder) they believe that the way to connect with women is through marketing-to-women. While marketing is a line function that touches all parts of the business, the minute you add "women" to the equation, somehow it becomes separate and apart. My 15 years of experience reveals that most marketing-to-women initiatives are simply variations of pink-washing—light, fluffy, and not to be taken at all seriously.

Women are demanding an entirely different business proposition than marketing-to-women. For retailers to put women at the centre of their business, they (read: people) need to change the lens or filter they use to see the world, which, frankly, is the only way to change the way one interacts with the world.

Depending on who you are, of course, this isn't really all that hard to do. In Chapter 4, we'll speak more about how leadership needs to adapt, but simply becoming conscious of the necessity for change is a huge first step. You live in the real world at home, on airplanes, in stores, watching TV, in restaurants, yacht clubs, health clubs, in hospitals, at baseball games, at your kid's soccer games. Look around and see how pervasive marketing-to-women is.

CREATING AN ORGANIC OR GENDER-INTELLIGENT RETAIL ECOSYSTEM

It doesn't matter where you or your company are on the gender-intelligence curve; there will be a mindset change required. An organic farmer views his or her farm as an organism in which the soil minerals, organic matter, micro-organisms, insects, plants, animals, and people are a coherent and stable whole. Is this how your company operates when it comes to understanding women's needs? Is your company operating as an integrated whole, or in silos or as a filing cabinet?

There are as many ways to interpret and apply Gender-Intelligent Retail Ecology (GIRE) as there are companies on the planet. Each will need to mould the principles to fit with its own goals and internal culture. The overall strategy will be the same for everyone, but individual tactics, indeed, will vary. The following is a blueprint of the steps toward this end.

Creating an Organic or Gender-Intelligent Retail Ecosystem
Step One: Develop an internal gender lens: Recognize gender differences that take women seriously
Step Two: Determine your company's current ecosystem: Where are you on the gender-intelligence continuum?
Step Three: Organizational readiness: Prepare to change your internal culture
Step Four: Develop an internal gender lens to identify and control PESTs:
■ *P*roduct or service development
■ *E*nvironment (store/office)
■ *S*ales tools (education, marketing, advertising)
■ *T*raining (face-to-face customer points of contact)

The first step to GIRE is achieving an *intelligent* perspective on how women and men are different. While fascinating and often hilarious, it's important to understand how these differences impact how a business should be run. This is crucial because the de facto model of business today is typically based on a male model or perspective since it's usually men designing stores and office spaces and making senior-level decisions. This in and of itself is not a bad thing if the leaders are gender intelligent. If they aren't, a one-dimensional, male world view will prevail. And though some would argue things are changing, most would state the world of retail is still very much a man's world.

While understanding gender differences seems like a pretty obvious place to start, the vast majority of companies tend to look at this very superficially. It might include throwing in a VCR and some Barney videos in the waiting room or involve a targeted mailing to "soccer moms," a term that most women consumers find offensive as hell. The next chapter offers insight into legitimate gender differences that manifest in consumer behaviour, something companies usually ignore. As we progress through the book, we'll show you a handful of companies that built their businesses on understanding and integrating these differences into their business models. They had strong, clear leadership that ensured the changes made were systemic or organic and sustainable over the long term. Their results may surprise you.

CHAPTER TWO

The Beaver and the Octopus

Men do not shop. Men buy. Women shop, which only means, "See what's available and make sure you see everything." They might make a purchase, they might not. This is why men don't go "shopping" with their wives or girlfriends. After five minutes of "Do you think these potholders will make the oven look fat?" most guys will never go near a store with a woman. Just one man's opinion . . .

—An online entry on a website

I recently came across some of the most hare-brained research on gender differences from the turn of the twentieth century that would have had me in stitches if it wasn't so alarming. Back then, it was believed that men's brains were physically larger, ergo the "superior" sex. This led to all kinds of really bad behaviour that resulted in women, at best, being patted on the head with the proverbial "There, there, dear" to being prohibited outright from fully participating in society through sports, politics, education, business, etc.

Today we know for a fact that men's brains are larger, but it doesn't mean a darn thing other than that they are, uh, larger. Men's bodies (which include their heads, the last time I looked) are also larger, therefore, Mother Nature intuitively knew she had to somehow fill up the space. But women and men both do just fine on IQ tests. Pretty much everyone has both male and female abilities and capabilities; it's just a question of the difference in the degree to which one set predominates. Gender differences are not mutually exclusive categories but operate on more of a continuum. Everyone has characteristics representative along that continuum, but research supports that more women than men think, act, consume, communicate a certain way, and vice versa. And, yes, women and men do often find themselves at opposite ends of that line. I like to describe gender differences this way: My husband and I are sitting in a theatre. We are seated side by side and appear to be looking at the same screen, yet we invariably end up watching two entirely different movies.

Suffice it to say that there are thousands of studies in fields as diverse as biochemistry and anthropology that prove and reconfirm that there are numerous gender-related differences between men and women. The question remains: "So what?" It's a pretty big question. Gender-based research is an exploding field and remains somewhat controversial today, though much less so than before. Most researchers seem to agree that women and men actually *are* biologically different. And no one whose address doesn't involve a cave can argue that we're different in terms of how little girls and boys are raised and viewed by society.

We're going to look at some of the key gender differences, both biological and sociological, that retailers need to know about. This will go well beyond the usual "Girls like pink, live longer, and are the child bearers of the species."

MEN EMULATE THE SINGLE-MINDED BEAVER

Studies indicate that men tend to distribute information processing throughout the brain. There is also a function that inhibits "information spread" in the cortex. It appears that men have the ability to turn off areas or distractions that could interfere with the work at hand. This allows a single-mindedness that is ideal for solving difficult spatial problems (like finding something in an old-style hardware store). This also explains why I can stand next to my husband, Michael, and call his name six times, but he doesn't hear me. It's only when I stick my finger in his ribs, stand back, and watch him vault to the ceiling that I'm able to get his attention.

Let's put this in a retail context. Dr. Raymond Burke, professor at the Retail Management School at the University of Kansas, noted the following in his observations of men and women shopping: Men tended to touch items at the front of the store, sweep through the store to the back of the clearance items (not touching anything in between), then head out the door. When exiting a store, men were asked why they didn't touch anything. Most said it was too hard to fold the products and put them back the same neat way. When the store adjusted products to make them more touchable, sales went up immediately for men's products. There was also much more product interaction throughout the store with women, who tended to cover more of the store's territory.

Women have more information processing occurring when they are shopping. They could put together more clothing combinations from different parts of the store that were not necessarily connected through the display. Women have more "professional" shopping behaviour and tend to be more organized and purposeful.

WOMEN EMULATE THE MULTITASKING OCTOPUS

Women's brains are more densely packed, which gives women a kind of concentrated processing power. Their brains have the capacity to link disparate thoughts and ideas together. (This is how women can take that bone-headed move their partner pulled nine years ago and make it relevant to this morning's argument.) In a retail context, women will want to see lots of options and can make connections that usually don't jibe with the linear thinking and approach of most retail environments. A good example of this is grouped displays. These tend to register with women and help to create important landmarks in a store. In Sean's experience, he says, "Men tend to see them as wallpaper. Men go to the rack [linear] whereas women visit a display [connective]."

MORE BEAVER AND OCTOPUS . . .

Women's brains are organized for multitracking, juggling an average of two to four unrelated topics at the same time. I (and most women I know) am very capable of listening to CBC Radio while talking on the telephone, listening to my daughter's conversation with her friend in the next room, and washing it all down with a cup of tea.

Barbra and Allan Pease, in their seminal work called *The Definitive Book of Body Language*, suggest that women can talk about several unrelated topics in one conversation and use five vocal tones to change the subject or emphasize points. Most men can't do this. (Most men don't want to.) What's also fascinating is that men seem to be biologically equipped to hear or identify only three of the five tones. (I suspect this ability to focus is evolutionary. One needs a certain level of concentration when stalking carnivores.) This reduced tone-recognition capacity may also contribute to women's very common complaint: "John, I don't think you are getting my meaning here." Male sales associates really need to triple-check that they have understood the request being asked. It's "sales 101" to always paraphrase the customer's response to check for understanding.

LANGUAGE SKILLS

Another important distinction between the sexes is that both sides of women's brains are more easily activated. Language resides on the right side of the brain and it appears to be more developed in women. (Women tend to score higher than men on difficult verbal tasks.) The stereotypical depiction of the salesperson "t-a-l-k-i-n-g s-l-o-w-l-y" to help explain the feature of a product is pretty annoying for anyone, but is especially annoying to women.

Magnetic resonance imaging (MRI) brain scans reveal why women have far greater capacity for communicating with and evaluating people than men. Women have, on average, between 14 and 16 areas of the brain to evaluate others' behaviour versus men's 4 to 6. At a dinner party, I can rapidly work out who had an argument before coming and who is flirting with whom.

A lot of customer service failures with women customers can be traced back to undercommunicating salespeople who leave too much open for interpretation. Comments such as "Your salespeople obviously don't care," can be the result of non-verbal cues being interpreted as a lack of concern. Active listening is a skill that requires a fair bit of dialogue, something we'll talk about in a later chapter.

SPATIAL DIFFERENCES

Gender differences in spatial cognition and language manifest in a myriad of ways: At the risk of sounding stereotypical, the truth remains that little girls tend to prefer more "people-like" dolls and playing house. Boys, on the other hand, like mechanical toys and blowing up houses. Men, especially in the workplace, will tend to order, whereas most women prefer to negotiate. Then there's my favourite: navigation. My husband Michael is an aerospace engineer. When someone gives him directions, I watch in complete amazement as he not only visualizes some kind of weird geometric system, he draws a map, complete with a North/South compass as he's being dictated the directions. I, on the other hand, will write out the words and personalize the route with landmarks.

Sean says he's noticed that when men enter a store, they zoom in on the product while women zero in on the salespeople. There are a couple of reasons for this. First, women don't want to waste time they don't have. Then, there is also the issue of creating social ease in the retail environment, which may not be user-friendly to begin with. "Generally, the pattern is that women find a salesperson, then go to the product, whereas men prefer to go to the product first, even if they don't know where it is. The classic conversation I overhear constantly is, Woman: 'Why don't we just ask a salesperson?' Man: 'No, it's okay. I'll just find it.'"

WOMEN'S X-RAY VISION

There is another layer of gender differences that has great relevance to retailers and service providers. Research shows that non-verbal signals carry about five times as much impact as verbal signals, and that when the two are incongruent, people—especially women—rely on the non-verbal messages and disregard the verbal content.[1] This is a non-verbal ticking time bomb for retailers, especially in

1   Allan and Barbra Pease, *The Definitive Book of Body Language* (New York: Bantam Dell, 2006), 23.

high-volume environments. The average high-volume retailer will see between 2,000–3,000 people come through the doors on a peak day. Sean adds, "While no one measures this specifically, generally speaking, between 50 and 70 percent of the traffic will be female, depending on the type of retailer."

Women, more so than men, it seems, are excellent at intuiting the feelings and thoughts of others, in essence "reading" people. We know that women notice and process the little things to a far greater degree and with greater frequency than men. Women notice the creases in your clothes, the tension in your voice, your tapping foot, the faint hint of annoyance on your lower lip. They pick up messages from posture, gestures, emotional expressions, and voice. Then, with their uniquely constructed brains, women are more apt to assimilate all of these disparate little facts faster, achieving what appears to be a clairvoyant view. Again, that can put a lot of pressure on a salesperson (or a husband).

It's not only about what you're selling, but how you're selling, with women noticing everything right down to a bad haircut.

Research by psychologists at Harvard University showed how women are far more alert to body language than men. They showed short films, with the sound turned off, of a man and woman communicating. The participants were asked to decode what was happening by reading the couple's expressions. The research showed that women read the situation accurately 87 percent of the time, while the men scored only 42 percent accuracy. "Female intuition" is particularly evident in women who have raised children. For the first few years, the mother relies almost solely on the non-verbal channel to communicate with the child, which is why women are often more perceptive negotiators than men. They practise reading signals early.[2]

EYE CONTACT IN THE NUDIST COLONY

The Peases tell a hilarious story in their book of sending a group of non-nudists to a nudist colony. They filmed where non-nudists were looking when they were introduced to new people. All the non-nudist men reported that they had trouble resisting the urge to look down and the video replay showed how obvious it was when they did look down. The women said they did not experience these problems and rarely were women filmed intentionally gazing toward the nether regions. This is because men are equipped with a form of tunnel vision that makes them far better than women at seeing directly in front of them and over long distances for spotting targets. Most men's close-range and peripheral vision is far poorer than women's, however, which is why men have difficulty seeing things in refrigerators, cupboards, and drawers. Women's peripheral vision extends to at least 45 degrees on each side, above and below, which means they can appear to be looking at someone's face while, at the same time, they are inspecting their goods and chattels.

THE THOUGHT PROCESS: WOMEN INTEGRATE, MEN ELIMINATE

Women seem to be hard-wired for a top-down, big-picture take. On average, they don't think in a linear, step-by-step fashion as men do. The process is more like webs of interrelated factors, not straight

---

2   Ibid., 13–14.

lines. Women explore the multiple interactions, the multidirectional paths, all the permutations of the puzzle. They consider more options and outcomes, recall more points of view, and see more ways to proceed. They integrate, generalize, and synthesize, and they tolerate ambiguity better than men do. They visualize more of the factors involved in any issue.

This typically means women may take longer to make decisions, but when they do, they are well thought out. It's one of the reasons women demonstrate a higher degree of loyalty to companies that have, in their view, performed well. Since women do so much upfront research, when they make a decision about a company, it's usually a pretty concrete, long-lasting one. Women's holistic brain capacity also means that retailers need to have their act together in terms of having an organic, integrated view of their business; advertising needs to mesh with merchandising strategy, and the sales strategy needs to interact with the Web strategy. Women are piecing it all together and determining whether it makes sense or is credible.

Most women have a 360-degree perspective on life and evaluate products and services by how they fit into that bigger picture. Men tend to be programmed to look at things from the bottom up with a more narrow view. They focus first on minute detail, and operate most easily with a certain detachment. They construct rules-based analyses of the natural world, inanimate objects, and events, and can easily systemize or compartmentalize. Men are more selective processors of information, who tend to pick up on single, highly salient, or personally relevant pieces of information that are quickly and easily processed. They disregard the rest. Look at how women and men buy technology. Research reveals that they both want a fair price, but men tend to be more concerned with processing power (How fast is it? How much memory can it store? etc.). Women, on the other hand, are primarily concerned with ease of use (How easy is it to get this running? How easy is it to use? Will someone help me if I have problems?).

It's as simple as retailers and service providers needing to communicate benefits in a relevant manner, in accordance with how men and women make decisions.

Think of it this way: This narrow-casting that men use in the retail setting is a process of elimination. Men tend to focus on one aspect at a time, rather than looking at the whole picture at once. This also has implications for retail display and product placement. Women will tend to view the whole aspect of the display first, while men will hone in quickly to individual products and focus on attributes that help eliminate it or others from the decision-making process. Women take in and process information quickly, but they also want to view the information in its entirety. They can go through a decision-making process, tracking a number of points, all at the same time. Some salespeople, especially men who have been trained to move through the hierarchy of choices in a progression of good-better-best, may view this as "erratic" decision making.

Sean has seen this first-hand. "One of the things that I have noticed in my retail experience is that when I work with women customers, they are much more likely than men to ask a question like 'What about that over there?' What this means to me is that they are seeking new information even while I have been informing them about a product they've asked about. I find this a little unnerving because it means that they have noticed new data that is not even within our immediate vicinity. This is much different from an interaction with a male customer, who tends to focus on what you are focused on and only moves on to something else at the point that you do. In a traditional sales environment, this can drive salespeople to distraction as their product training teaches them to go through the information in a linear fashion of good-better-best. Women seem to be constantly pulling in information from everywhere when you are trying to focus their attention. Consequently, salespeople can get thrown off. That's actually frustrating for both the salesperson and the customer."

One of our technical advisers on this book, Helen "Pit Bull" Bullingham (she is a brilliant but kamikaze-like editor), shares this story: "This very thing happened to me this past Saturday. I was at Staples getting a memory stick. The salesperson was showing me the top model (8 gigabytes) on the top shelf. I'm saying, 'What about this one over here?' (2 gigabytes), which was on the lowest shelf. I felt he was trying to sell me the top-priced model because he thought I didn't know much about memory sticks and, therefore, was attempting to beef up his commission. [*Author's note:* Staples doesn't work on commission.] When I told my husband, Dave, how I felt about this, he didn't agree. He said, 'No, he was simply starting with the best.'"

ADVERTISING IMPLICATIONS

Advertisers also need to recognize that the success of their ad campaigns often depends on the judgments and knowledge that consumers assimilate from ads. Men are less interested in taking in every detail and may not be as prone to process layers of mixed or complicated messages and images. With women, advertisements can provide more information, encourage inference, and need not be literal. Women are likely to read between the lines and to read an ad or watch a commercial all the way through, and they tend to remember and retrieve the message easily, *assuming* that they've made relevant mental associations in the process.[3]

WHO'S EMOTIONAL?

Another interesting gender difference is that women are considered more emotional than men. However, studies suggest that emotion is driven by context. Women are more emotional in an interpersonal context, and men are more emotional in an achievement context.

Look at shampoo commercials. My personal favourite is the 10-year-old ad campaign showing women in a variety of public washrooms, having orgasms while washing their hair. Then there's the very popular ad exhorting you to use this shampoo and the man of your dreams will come into your life (usually in a Jaguar). Men's shampoo ads usually feature some Super Bowl quarterback standing confidently in the centre of the page with a shot of a single shampoo bottle next to a slogan about winning. It's simple and direct, and it tells the reader that a champion uses this product. Both feel dumb and inauthentic to me, but the point is women are being targeted through the emotional context of interpersonal dynamics and men through an emotional context of achievement, winning, and perseverance. Marketers have got the gender-emotion part right, but it's their execution that is lacking.

---

3   Joanne Thomas Yaccato, *The 80% Minority* (Penguin Canada, 2003), 11–54.

WOMEN SEE THE GLASS HALF-EMPTY

This last biological gender difference is a killer for retailers. Women, it appears, are set up biologically to internally amplify their negative life experiences. Women's attention to detail and their way of processing contribute to why they are more likely to elaborate on any negative emotions, rather than on any positive emotions they feel at the time they make a purchase. Research points to this factor translating into greater trend effects (the negative is emphasized more over time if the process or evaluation is repeated), with women showing greater trend effects for negative emotions and men showing greater trend effects for positive emotions. Simply put, it appears women may be more inclined to look for the downside of the experience. Besides not being taken seriously or, worse, feeling that they are not being seen at all, women also have a finely tuned biological radar to pick this up.

WORD-OF-MOUTH

Word-of-mouth is an extremely powerful tool in retail. Bad word-of-mouth, especially among women's sophisticated jungle telegraph, can sink a retailer. Imagine that every woman who walks through the door actually represents 10 other potential customers. You are not just interacting with one woman standing in front of you, but her entire social network, as well.

If there was ever a case for adopting a gender-intelligent eco-system, this is it. This negative trend effect is also one of the major reasons why if you make something women-friendly, you make it everybody-friendly. Since women consumers have a biological

---

(Continued)

propensity to look for what's wrong in a consumer experience, their process for approval is generally more rigorous than men's. If you pass muster, you can be assured you've done something right and will have invariably improved the experience for everyone.

Since women show greater trend effects than men for negative emotions during the purchase process, while men show greater trend effects on the positive side of the ledger, it's crucial to check on customer satisfaction with women consumers to ensure that any negative feelings are dealt with immediately. Said another way, when women have a negative experience, 96 percent don't complain to the source—they just don't go back.[4] If for no other reason than this, the old expression of *caveat emptor* had better be extended to include "marketer beware."

THE NURTURE SIDE OF THE COIN

There's another important element of the gender differences discussion. There are clearly biological differences, but what about the ones that are taught? Social factors play a huge part in how the sexes interact with the world, things like women being society's child bearers and primary caregivers. There's also having grown up as what journalist Michele Landsberg famously coined as "objects of the gaze." There are consumer realities, such as women doing most of the family's purchasing. Mallika Das, professor of marketing at Mount Saint Vincent University, says, "Since women are the major purchasers of household items and food, general

---

4   Ibid.

household shopping is considered part of a woman's role. As a result, girls are given more purposeful consumer/shopping training than boys. Men, on the other hand, are considered more specialist shoppers." Throw into the mix women's perception of not being taken seriously, frequently paying more than men for many of the same products or services, being so time-pressed that consumer behaviour is often dictated by who or what makes life simplest, and you'll soon see that gender differences ain't all about the genes.

As usual, nothing is cut and dried and some of these sociological differences have actually declined with time. The decrease correlated with women entering the workplace en masse, as well as men becoming more open about how they "feel" about things.

IT STARTS YOUNG

Consciously or unconsciously, we teach boys and girls to behave differently. I grew up hearing children's stories that had a boy as almost every central character and where the top two occupations for girls were housewife and witch. There are two areas where gender-based socialization has a huge impact on consumer behaviour: (1) child/elder and home care, and (2) being the keeper of society's small "l" liberal values.

THE TRUTH ABOUT TIME

Whatever women's occupations are, they're usually CEO at home. Here's proof. As I sit here and write this, I've also managed to finagle my husband into coming with me at lunchtime to pick out the Christmas tree. I've taken out something for dinner, called the hairdresser to reschedule my appointment, fed the dog, wrote my daughter a note for school, checked out a new PowerPoint presentation, and scanned in a yearbook photo for a high school alumni site that I started. That's within the last 30 minutes. My husband is upstairs in his home office, working diligently away. Just working. At one thing.

Am I unusual? Absolutely not. But I am tired, as are most other women I know. Today, women are required to carry additional responsibilities that most of their mothers didn't. I love Erma Bombeck's classic musing on housework, "My second-favorite household chore is ironing. My first being hitting my head on the top bunk bed until I faint."

According to Statistics Canada, the increased complexity of women's role has led to higher levels of time stress, particularly for married parents aged 25–44 who are employed full-time. Compared with their counterparts without children living at home, married mothers with full-time jobs are twice as likely to be severely time-stressed (38 percent versus 26 percent). In contrast, there was no difference in the incidence of time stress for employed married men with or without children.

Women comprise almost half of the paid labour force, yet remain the dominant constituency of the unpaid labour force. Said another way, women have two full-time jobs. Statistics Canada reveals that every day, Canadian women in the paid labour force perform two hours more of child and home care—over and above their jobs—than their male counterparts. The 1999 United Nations *Human Development Report* states that women around the world perform the equivalent of US $3 trillion of unpaid work each year.[5]

---

5   United Nations Development Programme, *Human Development Report* (New
     York: Oxford University Press, 1999).

Double duty is having a pronounced effect on women's health. Chloe Bird, a researcher from Brown University, studied the impact of the amount of household labour performed and its division within the household on the levels of depression among men and women.[6] She concluded that men's lower contributions explain part of women's higher depression levels which is about unequal division of household labour. Other research reveals this double duty is also responsible for increases in heart disease among women. Job strain was characterized by a combination of heavy demands and little decision-making power, while stress at home came principally from having a high proportion of child-care responsibilities relative to one's partner. When we say women are busy, as these studies reveal, it is not a trite statement.

Saving time is a myth. There is and always will be only 24 hours in a day and everyone gets the same 24 hours, no matter what. Women won't believe you if you tell them you will save them time. Saving time only means more time to do something else. However, what you can do is make life *simpler*. Women just don't have the time to wander aimlessly through aisles or sit in waiting rooms. Bullingham says, "The implications for me are, that start to finish, the retail experience is wholly unsatisfying. I don't have time, the salesperson isn't giving me the information the way I want it, they are elevating my stress—NO ONE IS HELPING ME!"

---

6   Chloe E. Bird, "Gender, Household Labor, and Psychological Distress: The Impact of the Amount and Division of Housework," *Journal of Health and Social Behaviour* 40 (1999).

WOMEN'S KEY CONSUMER STANDARDS

How to Make Women's Lives Simpler

- Make house calls where appropriate. (Women will often pay extra for this convenience.)

- Resolve service issues quickly—make sure it takes only one call. One of our technical advisers told us of a friend who bought a gift at Sporting Life. When she got home, she discovered the security tag was left on it. She called and they actually sent someone to her house that afternoon to take it off. They also gave her a gift card toward her next purchase. She lived a considerable distance from the store as well. Pretty impressive.

- Combine, complement, and reuse information, products, and services: Only one form instead of several, only one request to enter mailing information, only one lineup.

- Eliminate unnecessary steps, confusing instructions, and delays and errors.

- Determine what is really necessary: Are all those forms, rules, and lineups even required?

- Consider e-tailing and extended hours of operation.

- Provide choices for services, delivery, and packaging so women have control over how, when, where, how much, and by whom.

- Make helping to manage time a key message in advertising and marketing material.

A Woman's Multidimensional Lens

- Is what you are selling a real or a pumped-up image?

(Continued)

- Does it authentically reflect a woman's world? The people in her life? Her family?

- Does it provide support for a woman's many roles or can it serve only one need?

- Does your customer service support a relationship-oriented process?

- Does it support women's role as primary caregivers?

- Does it support women's role as a parent, whether single or not?

- Does it satisfy women's demand for information?

- Does it help women share information?

- Does it offer a win/win outcome, ethical solution, or do good?

- Do the benefits have an impact on issues important to women, namely, social, health, financial, and environmental issues?

USE A HOLISTIC HEALTH LENS

The other nurture piece is the lens through which women view the world. Women tend to be society's small "l" liberals. Our research revealed that 60 percent of women will change brand to support the environment. Statistics Canada shows that more women than men are involved in volunteerism. Women are the impetus behind the organic food movement and alternative health care movements, and the flashpoints for the increase in yoga and other health- and fitness-related trends. Women make up most of the retail ethical investors in North America.

Research also shows that historically and, arguably, today, women tend to be society's social conscience and the keepers of social values. They tend to still be at the centre of the hearth and home and are the primary influencers of home purchases and decisions regarding children's education. Essentially, women remain the primary providers of their family's sustenance, both inside and out, including the soul life and the more physical needs, such as food, and physical and emotional health.

The net effect of this is that women see the world through a wide-angle health lens, one that encompasses family, physical, emotional, spiritual, environmental, and financial dimensions. Rarely are decisions made that aren't reviewed through this filter.

Very few retailers get this. While women don't have much of a choice as they need to shop somewhere, retailers and service providers lose out on soft benefits such as word-of-mouth.

SO HERE'S THE "SO *WHAT*?" PART

These are but only some of the major differences between women and men and how we view, live, and breathe in our respective worlds, but they are hugely relevant and core to the issues that retailers have with women. The retail experience, from the website to the face-to-face encounter, from market research to product development, is often based on men's world view. The start of a gender-intelligent approach to retailing is not focused on trying to make the experience more feminine, but on what is driving the purchasing decision for women and integrating it into the entire process.

Sean, our resident retail head, has taken his years of experience of selling to women and created a list of his educated observations.

**SEAN'S LIST OF WHAT YOU NEED TO KNOW
ABOUT WOMEN CONSUMERS**

1. Women tend to demonstrate more inquisitiveness in products and their uses. Their integration process (collecting all available information) is more lengthy than men's elimination process (streamlining available information), which means women will take up more of a salesperson's time. This also means retailers need to show more respect for women's process. Often a salesperson will start a "complex" sale without understanding the timetable, leading to an unsatisfactory experience. By checking in on time constraints and asking permission to engage in the sales process up front, you show the woman consumer that her time is being valued.

2. Women are more willing to look at lateral ideas to solve problems and are generally more open to alternatives. Men have a tunnel vision that does not allow for easy adoption of other options. With women, you will likely have more of a dialogue while they process information. It may feel like you are bouncing around, going over previously covered information. It is a bit more cut and dried with men. Sean explains: "It's almost like you have one opportunity to go through the product information. Once the product has been eliminated from the decision-making process, many men are reluctant to have it reintroduced."

3. Women take a more comprehensive look at how a product is made or fits, as well as warranty and after-sales service. Women are less focused on the pure transactional exchange of x for y, but more on the broader attributes of the sale. The warranty and after-sales aspects of a product or service become part of the "How will you take care of me when things go wrong?"

(Continued)

4. Women have high expectations of fit and performance. They don't want the product to be a compromise of men's design, but expect it to be designed specifically for them. This is not about simply the fit being flattering, but that some thought has gone into how a product will work for women. Fit is not just about apparel. The principle applies to all products to a certain extent.

5. Women are receptive to learning, but are active and involved learners. As women enter new markets and product areas, the retailer will need to fill the knowledge gap that may exist. Women tend to want the know-how upfront rather than learn by doing (a classic male approach). Women rarely have the time or budget to make mistakes.

6. Women want to get full explanations and to understand the technical details of a product, but in ways that are *relevant*. The retailer is a translator. Most products are conceived, designed, and delivered to market by men. That puts the retailer in the role of the intermediary, who needs to translate this information into relevant terms for women. This is often mistaken for a pandering, dumbing-down approach, which is equivalent to speaking English louder when you are in a foreign country.

7. In a retail environment, women spend more time and look with more determination than men, which increases your opportunity to make a sale. But it also means that you as a retailer need to know that women pay attention to the minute details of a store's environment.

8. Women look for and expect more customization and delivery of a service that meets their needs. This requires more flexibility from retailers, who need to look for more creative ways to deliver service, especially ways to make women's lives simpler.

(Continued)

9. Women generally have high expectations of error recovery and warranty process. It's not easy to meet expectations, let alone exceed them, but if you figure this out, the payback is huge. Our publisher described an experience with the Apple Store where she had to return a defective product. The return process was so slick that it actually made her *more* enthusiastic about recommending the product even though the original one failed.

Sean has discovered that when these issues are addressed, it's a win/win for everyone. Focusing on creating a women-friendly experience invariably works for both genders. This is the heart and soul of a gender-intelligent retail ecosystem.

CHAPTER THREE

Going Beyond 2 × 4s and Nails

In the past decade or so, the women's magazines have taken to
running home-handyperson articles suggesting that women
can learn to fix things just as well as men. These articles are
apparently based on the ludicrous assumption that men know
how to fix things, when in fact all they know how to do is
look at things in a certain squinty-eyed manner, which they
learned in Wood Shop; eventually, when enough things in the
home are broken, they take a job requiring them to transfer
to another home.

—Dave Barry, Humour Columnist

We're going to kick-start your synapses by giving you a tangible, real-life illustration of the concepts of *organic, gender-intelligent ecosystems,* and *retail ecology.* Before a company can transform the customer experience, it needs to understand the customer. From women's point of view, herein lies the problem: The vast majority of companies view the customer experience through a generic lens.

The Home Depot Canada, led by president Annette Verschuren, is in the process of transforming itself from a company practising monoculture to one that is incorporating organic principles by using, among other things, a gender lens. Today, women are responsible for half of all purchases made at The Home Depot, and the transformation is resulting in significant sales increases—not surprising, as single women are the number-one home purchasers in Canada and influence most of what gets purchased in the home.

Verschuren's predecessor had lamented the state of the home-improvement world and had capped the company's store growth potential at 19 stores, retiring with $700 million in annual sales. Today, there are 167 Home Depot stores in Canada. Every one of these stores has Verschuren and her team's stamp all over them. Revenues are now more than $6 billion.

The purpose of this case study is to show the merits of adopting gender-intelligent retail ecology, illustrate how The Home Depot is making the transition, and give you ideas on how your company can start making the necessary change. Here are some of the realities Verschuren faced when beginning her company's transition:

- Women are responsible for 70 percent of home-renovation projects, yet . . .
- Three times more women than men have experienced a retail situation where they felt they were being treated less seriously because of their gender.
- Women are less satisfied than men with their customer experience in the home-renovation industry.
- Women don't buy "products," they invest in "projects."
- "Making life simpler" resonates much more strongly with women than men.
- Women aren't keen to shop in a warehouse/lumberyard store esthetic.
- While corporate stewardship is important to both women and men, it is a much greater driver of loyalty for women than it is for men.

- Sixty percent of women will change a brand to support the environment.
- Women look for macro-level benefits, whereas men respond more to speeds and feeds. Stating the physical, emotional, or spiritual health benefits of products or services is much more likely to capture the attention of women.
- Women, more so than men, want to see an accurate reflection of their lives in a retailer's approach to advertising, products, services, and store design.
- Oh yes, did we mention that Lowe's, one of the bright spots in women-friendly retailing, was moving into Canada? Lowe's has set an impressive standard and The Home Depot had a l-o-o-o-n-g way to go to live up to it.

These gender-based consumer differences are precisely what Verschuren had to consider when transitioning The Home Depot retail ecosystem. The bottom line? Adopting gender-intelligent retail ecology will increase sales by ensuring that women consumers feel their needs are understood and that they are being taken seriously.

CASE STUDY: THE HOME DEPOT CANADA

I'm always struck by how Verschuren speaks about her childhood. She recounts her upbringing with the same pride as her well-documented successes at The Home Depot. Annette Verschuren is the daughter of Tony and Annie Verschuren, proud Cape Breton dairy farmers whose family lived in Upper North Sydney. When Tony suffered a heart attack in 1966, Annie and their five children took over the farm work. To make things more manageable and to increase crop quality and yields, the

Verschuren farm went organic, which meant a complete overhaul in farming techniques.

This transitioning experience became the genesis of Verschuren's lifelong proclivity to buck the system and to look at situations in a new way by developing a gender/ecological filter that she uses to this day.

Prior to Verschuren taking over the reins at The Home Depot Canada, there were very few women working or shopping in The Home Depot stores, and none at all in the boardroom. Verschuren explains: "This was a closed, old boys' network. Retail and wholesale attitudes melded into each other." She knew that things needed to change fast. She wanted to swing her team and the organization around to a holistic, customer-focused company, one that used women consumers as its filter and its anchor. Says Verschuren, "Since women were an underserved customer, we added women to our already existing lens that focused on men and the pros. That meant women's perspectives and needs, along with everyone else's, were now included in merchandising, training, store design, product selection, and PLP strategy development." Verschuren adds, "It's still a boys' store. But there are places that women spend more time, and places that men spend more time."

Step One: Determine Your Company's Current Ecosystem—Where Are You on the Gender-Intelligence Continuum?

Verschuren simply *knew* that there was business beyond 2×4s and nails. During her first visit to a Home Depot store in her new capacity as boss, she was struck by the fact that, even though she stood there for over four hours, she hadn't seen a single woman, including one working at the store. It was easy to see where the company resided on the gender-intelligence continuum.

In order to transition to a gender-intelligent retail ecosystem, Verschuren recognized that a company needed a gender lens, one that included both women and men, especially since her business was dominated by men in the first place. While she quickly realized it was just as important to look at men's evolving roles, her emphasis needed to be on women since they are the missing piece.

"I knew women were hugely involved in home renovations and yet the female side of our business was seriously underrepresented," she says, still shaking her head in bewilderment.

Verschuren believes transitioning a conventional company culture is the same process as a conventional farm moving to organic. "The first step is to understand exactly where you are so you know where you have to go." We will deal with this in detail in Chapter 4, but there are four primary retail ecosystems within a hierarchy:

1. *Conventional:* Business as usual, monoculture
2. *Evolved conventional:* Accidental gender intelligence or not "strategic"
3. *Transitional:* Conscious gender lens being adopted throughout the company
4. *The gender-intelligent retail ecosystem:* The goal

In order to see where The Home Depot was in the hierarchy, Verschuren needed to ask herself and her team some tough questions.

CORPORATE GENDER-INTELLIGENCE AUDIT: FIVE QUESTIONS TO ASK YOURSELF

1. How is our company/industry perceived by women consumers?

2. Do men consumers perceive the company/industry as one that meets the needs of women consumers?

3. Is the company motivated by profits rather than sustainability?

4. Does the company acknowledge that women are valuable customers with distinct needs?

5. Does the company use a gender lens or filter consistently and holistically when making key strategic decisions? When hiring? When developing products? When conducting market research? When designing stores and making merchandising decisions? Through all its communications?

Historically, The Home Depot was a company run by men, selling to men. However, Verschuren knew that if she was going to appeal to women consumers, it was pretty clear the organization needed to move from its conventional "stack 'em high and watch 'em fly" and the good-better-best hammer-and-drill approach to retailing. She went to the head office in Atlanta with her proposal.

The reaction to her idea to focus on women consumers not only ruffled a few feathers, but also seriously tested Verschuren's mettle. Though she had some key support, there were many others who believed this "women thing" was fluff and frivolity. In her own words, "Challenging the way business was run worked for my dad and it worked and continues to work for me. There were certain smart businessmen who saw the future potential of women as an important customer base, so I received the sponsorship to pursue it. However, other senior guys in the organization gave the concept a rough ride. It was a very lonely transition, but I was tough enough to keep the filter."

Step Two: Organizational Readiness—Preparing to Change Your Internal Culture

Like her father before her, Verschuren realized that transitioning to organic principles was not just something you *did*, it was something you *became*. Her internal gender lens was responsible

---

ASSESSING ORGANIZATIONAL READINESS

1. Is there a champion of the change at the executive table? If the CEO is not the change champion, is he or she aligned with these efforts?

2. Are the leaders, both women and men, aware of systemic, male-based processes and perspectives within the company?

3. Are the leaders of the organization willing to hold up and examine the company's sacred cows?

4. Can the leaders put their money where their mouth is? In other words, will there be people and financial resources committed to creating a gender-intelligent retail ecosystem?

5. Are the leaders prepared to be consistent and strategic? Are they creating a companywide core competency or are they treating this as a marketing-to-women event?

6. Are the leaders ready to make the systemic changes needed— change scorecards, update training and evaluation systems—to properly recognize and reward new behaviours that will drive and sustain the change?

7. Are women decision makers represented throughout the organization?

8. How ready is the organization for change? How ready are the leaders?

for the many questions that percolated around getting the company ready for this shift.

Once she figured out the answers, Verschuren began the process of ridding the company of its monoculture. She recruited really, really smart people, people who already "got diversity" so that they could help carry the banner. Her view is that if fundamental core values exist in a person, then concepts like gender intelligence are teachable. But whatever change you expect to make needs to mesh with existing company values.

The plan was to create a diverse management team to lead a diverse organization that would appeal to a diverse customer base. Another central part of her strategy to change company mindset was to give women a voice in the boardroom and in the stores. Verschuren is pretty sure that The Home Depot boasts the highest percentage of women merchants/buyers in the industry.

She is also adamant that her work as the company change agent rises above any one champion or market condition. It took her five years to make serious headway toward making women employees and consumers intrinsic to company processes and procedures. That's the legacy Verschuren wants to leave behind. The greatest challenge remains satisfying many different customers under one roof and continuing to evolve to reflect diversity in the ever-changing Canadian culture.

Verschuren was smart enough to know that gender intelligence is also about the capacity to *implement* what is learned while using the gender lens. Sometimes it's as simple as putting change tables in men's washrooms, one of the many moves The Home Depot made. Today, you see products grouped together in a way that you would think of them—light bulbs with light fixtures and so on. Other times it can mean a complete corporate overhaul, especially if the culture is a true monoculture, something more common than you'd like to think.

Related to the capacity to implement is the corporate soul of the company. Corporate responsibility and business practices, especially regarding the environment, are important to the majority of women and men, but remember that these factors are much greater drivers of loyalty for women. Our research revealed that women are more observant of company practices and how well they match with the company's image. Verschuren realized that a significantly higher number of women than men would change brand to support the environment. She was also acutely aware that women tend not to want to deal with large, faceless, anonymous companies anymore. They look for a community connection, both local and global, and in a variety of ways: women on the board of directors as well as on the sales floor or in the sales office, responsible environmental practices, fair employment practices, and the like.

The Home Depot has shown great community leadership in a myriad of different ways. Internally, there is a Women's Affinity Group that shares the women's experiences and opens the doors for communication across the organization and fosters mentoring opportunities. The group, run exclusively by women, develops their own plans of action, which are supported by the organization. Men in management are also mentoring women managers.

Step Three: Develop an Internal Gender Lens—Taking Women Seriously by Recognizing Consumer-Relevant Gender Differences

While our research showed there are no differences between women and men in terms of gender preference of salespeople, it pretty much ends there. Verschuren's instinct guided her toward the one universal and most serious complaint that women consumers have: They do not feel that they are taken seriously. Verschuren knew this was to be fundamental to *everything* that The Home Depot embarked on to reach out to women consumers. Women didn't want to be treated "like men." If that were true, why bother changing anything? This was precisely what was happening in the stores every day. And this is core to gender intelligence: Women consumers don't want to be treated *like* men, *they want to be taken as seriously as men.*

Women live as multidimensional thinkers in a unidimensional retail world. When we say women are multidimensional, we generally mean two things:

1. Women's brains are constructed in such a way that everything they process is somehow connected to something else. It also affects how women shop in a big way. Multidimensional also means a higher capacity for multitasking. Verschuren was really clear that women gravitate to a solution-oriented approach, which means offering lots of choices. Ask yourself: Is your store intuitive to shop in? Do your product displays make sense? How does your product make lives simpler? What are physical, mental, spiritual, or financial benefits? You'll further reach customers by applying these answers to product engineering and development, how and where you market, and your delivery channels, store hours, customer support, and how you position your merchandise so that it has an impact. As Verschuren astutely observes, "You can sell sinks, vanities, toilets, tubs, and faucets or you can sell an oasis of calm and relaxation in your home."

2. Women, much more so than men, want to see an accurate reflection of their life and world view in a retailer's approach to advertising, products, services, and store design. Companies that articulated and demonstrated product or service benefits through a physical, emotional, spiritual, financial, and environmental health lens were much more likely to capture the attention of women. Women are more likely than men to seek out retailers that consider their family needs. "Make my life simpler" was a key message from women, one that resonated much more strongly with women than men.

I shared with Verschuren a Home Depot shopping experience that I had a few years back that spoke to both of these points. I went into the store to purchase something very specific in mind, but as usual, got sidetracked as I wandered through the aisles. There was a build-it-yourself, multicoloured wooden chest on display. However, it took an hour to find all of the bits and pieces needed to put the foolish thing together. The chest kit was in one department, paint in another, sandpaper in yet another, and so it went. While everyone is time-pressed these days, women are disproportionately so. I, like most women, really resent wasting time I don't have, especially when it is completely unnecessary. All that was required was to have everything I needed to put this chest together in one place near the display. Simple.

Here was a perfect example of the lack of a gender lens. Men tend to go in with a list (read: plan) and rarely deviate from that plan. Women go in with a list, but it's just a suggested guideline. What leaders like Verschuren understand well is the following:

APPLYING A GENDER LENS TO THE CUSTOMER EXPERIENCE

- How do we create an experience that is an accurate reflection of women's lives in our approach to advertising, products, services, and store design?

- Are we providing women with solutions rather than selling products?

- What can we do throughout the entire customer experience to make women's lives simpler?

- How do we articulate what we sell through a macro-level health lens?

Top of the list for Verschuren and her team was creating an experience that was not in any way patronizing or pink-washed. The key to this was internalizing that it's about the experience, not adding senseless frills. They began to build on a core belief system that women would feel they were taken seriously if they saw a sales process, store environment, products, services, and amenities that reflected their life reality and provided solutions to their problems. This needed to be evident throughout the entire shopping experience, from the website through to the lumberyard. The mandate was to let women know that The Home Depot was no longer a warehouse selling products, but rather a legitimate consumer experience offering solutions.

Step Four: Develop an Internal Gender Lens to Identify and Control PESTs

Pests can wreak havoc not only in farming, but also in retail. In retail, PESTs is an acronym for:

- *P*roduct or service development
- *E*nvironment (store/office)
- *S*ales and communication tools (education, marketing, advertising)
- *T*raining (face-to-face customer points of contact)

Product or Service Development

In retail, one particularly annoying pest or weakness is product or service development that doesn't take women's needs into account. From The Home Depot's perspective, Verschuren and her team made sure women's preferences were considered by ensuring that their merchants and merchandisers have a gender lens when selecting products for the stores. She explains: "Women buy like they dress. They will buy the suit (the main project), then add accessories like jewellery, etc. They do the same when they renovate their home." Verschuren adopted a standard colour palette that was made available to all of the department merchandisers so continuity exists throughout. Today, bath hardware has the same finish as the faucets.

Another very interesting result of adopting a gender lens was the environmental approach the company now takes. Verschuren explains: "I spoke with hundreds of women and I figured out a key way to reach them not only included speaking in their language, but using an environmental dialect and offering environmentally sound choices as well." The Home Depot was the first major home-improvement retailer to embrace the importance of bringing environmental choices into the retail mix.

"With this in mind, we created the *Eco Options* magazine, a blend of content, product, and lifestyle features. The instantly recognizable style, tone, and spirit are part of our company's efforts to engage women, parents, and customers hungry for better choices. In fact, the format was consciously created to resonate with women consumers, but at the same time deliver practical advice on how small, everyday actions can help improve the environment." *Eco Options* has now grown into a year-round commitment, with a product line of more than 1,500 items.

Environment (Store/Office)

Verschuren and her team had the monumental headache of making a big-box warehouse that sold lumber into a place where women wanted to come and spend money. Eliminating that lumberyard mentality and redefining home improvement was no easy feat. Sean observes: "Historically, the design challenge for stores like The Home Depot was a store environment designed to sell building supplies in a very linear fashion. It reflected a layout that made sense from a Home Depot store buyer's perspective. It was also a design that was built around the efficiency of moving in and out of the building."

Many changes were made in store design and layout, including brighter lights, lower shelves to make things more accessible, wider aisles, as well as an offering of soft goods such as art and area rugs. The washrooms were moved from the back of the 3,987-acre stores up to the front, where women could access them quicker. (Smaller bladders mean much more frequent trips to the washroom.) Merchandise was cleared away from the entrance to the store and there's a wall with signage highlighting key promotions with copies of flyers. The seminar area of the store was rejuvenated to create a more customer-friendly environment. The stores were reduced from 110,000 square feet to 95,000 square feet to become more customer friendly. Home decor and paint boutiques were added.

Verschuren explains: "You know, women do shop differently. Because of that, we decided to take home decor products, complete kitchen displays, flooring, and windows and doors and placed them together in the centre of the store to offer a more holistic presentation. We even differentiated this area from the rest of the store with carpet. I also realized the importance of colour in our strategy to reach women. I saw the connection between what was on the runways in Paris and what showed up in the home six months later." This was a radical departure in thinking for a company with a bright orange logo and concrete warehouses for stores.

Recognizing women's time poverty, Verschuren also began to streamline to build in better efficiencies. Marketing, e-commerce, and community and public relations moved under one umbrella. Store planning and visual merchandising were coupled with merchandising to ensure a consistent look and feel and logical merchandise adjacencies. Installation services, supply chain management and asset protection were merged with operations.

Sales Tools (Education, Marketing, Advertising)

The concept of promotion is crucial, but it had to be organic or gender intelligent and it was this mindset that Verschuren brought to The Home Depot. Before she arrived, the company was killing the market with radio ads that were clearly developed in the US. The ads weren't only irrelevant to women, they were irrelevant to Canadians in general. They did very little to entice anyone to shop at the stores. People who "got" what they sold were plumbers, electricians, and renovators. The challenge for Verschuren was also to make The Home Depot culturally relevant while integrating the gender lens into development strategy. Verschuren explains: "They were building this awful male-dominated public persona. There was nothing for women. They had the ugliest flyers I've ever seen, something about an Aitkenhead Superman. Husbands loved them. Of course, when I started to use a gender lens on marketing material, there was controversy—'Why would you want to do this? If it ain't broke, why fix it?'—that sort of thing."

Verschuren and her team wanted to create something that was project-focused rather than product-focused, something they knew would resonate with women. She muses: "It was a struggle to find money to finance *The Dream Book*, something I knew would attract women. I wanted something they would keep on the coffee table, like the IKEA catalogue, so it had to be aspirational and inspirational." *The Dream Book* is focused on the interior and it helps customers visualize the whole room. Because of *The Dream Book* exercise, a gender lens became an integral part of all promotional development. The catalogue was responsible for a 20 percent sales lift in all of the areas it was distributed in.

Verschuren and her team also had the unenviable task of taking the organization from a purely transaction-based process to one that demonstrates total benefits. The company shifted from a product focus to a project focus, something multidimensional thinkers particularly value. It started with *The Dream Book*, but moved on to buying guides that describe products, highlight different styles, explain the benefits, and provide details and tips for the do-it-yourself project on Homedepot.ca. Another important shift for the company was offering specialty items for individual customer segments.

Women are avid consumers of information and advice. In fact, gathering information and doing research is a defining characteristic of women's consumer behaviour. Verschuren explains: "Women look for more and different types of information than men do. Men tend to like the technology, speed, and power thing. Women aren't as interested in that stuff. They want to know how this thing will make life better."

The Thomas Yaccato Group did a gender-lens store analysis for The Home Depot and one of the many things we looked at was the type of information used with product displays. Not surprisingly, it was pretty much all torque and BTUs. We recommended including more benefit-oriented information—making things environmentally friendly, how a product will make life simpler, that kind of thing. Even navigating through a store came under scrutiny: How easy was it to manoeuvre around the store with the information provided?

With this lens in place, the stores now offer consistent store maps to help customers navigate more easily. There are clean, crisp, and colourful images, both directional and inspirational. "Because women like it, I show pictures in my store much more. Our product brochures now include pictures that tell stories," says Verschuren.

The company's Eco Options signage identifies greener choices through consistent branding that also highlights the benefits, such as the cost and energy savings of using compact fluorescent light bulbs. New vendor signage guidelines were put in place to ensure that product signs are not only standardized but clean, crisp, and directional. Verschuren explains: "We also work very closely with the vendor community, designing merchandising sets with them. The gender lens is now benefiting them."

Training (Face-to-Face Customer Points of Contact)

While providing information is essential, so is the person providing it. Matching sales training to the customers' needs is an enormous pest, according to Verschuren. From a woman consumer's perspective, there is no greater area in need of a gender lens than this. Our study revealed that 65 percent of women versus 40 percent of men said they could tell if a company understood their needs by the way a salesperson talked to them. This should strike the fear of God into any rational-thinking sales trainer. Unless a gender lens is used in training sales associates, the issue of not being taken seriously will continue unabated.

Verschuren wanted to make sure that the folks on the floor understood how women shopped differently. The company became better at understanding the full cycle of influences and decisions in the purchase cycle. The Home Depot's leadership mantra, "create inclusion," is something the company looks for during the interview process. (For example, there are actually 19 different languages spoken in their Gerrard Square store in Toronto.)

"When everything is the same, you can't react to the differences," explains Verschuren. The Home Depot's leadership team didn't reflect the culture of the Canadian market they were trying to serve. In response, she took a United Nations approach to recruiting and screening. It became an almost self-selecting process. Verschuren explains: "Typically people don't want to work in a place if they don't share its corporate values. Because of this approach, I maintain we have the best retail associates in the industry."

The Home Depot takes training seriously, with 65 trainers working the field. All associates receive training on how to sell the project as a whole, which helps the customer understand all the components that go into making his or her home-improvement dreams a successful reality.

Verschuren saw first-hand that training needed to be ongoing. She says, "Good managers are able to realize what skills they need to improve on." Part of the cultural shift for The Home Depot team came in the form of a training program that we put executives through. The idea was to put people through perspective-expanding exercises to help decision makers get a better grip on women's consumer DNA. The centrepiece of the executive training occurs when executives are morphed into Laura, a 37-year-old mother of a newborn. To that end, everyone is suited up with baby snugglies, strollers, car seats, diaper bags, and purses, along with 10-pound babies, the kind that are used in schools to teach family planning. Then we tell everyone to go shopping in his or her own store.

Of course, a mystery-store shop has been set up so the "challenged" areas are known in advance. There was one classic "aha" moment that Verschuren and I often laugh about. The operations guy, Bob, was wearing the infant snuggly on his chest with his "baby" tucked safely inside. While manoeuvring that huge, cumbersome shopping cart, some keener staff kid whipped around the corner, not paying attention, and clipped the front end of his cart. There was an audible gasp from the group when his "baby" got crushed. (At that moment, we witnessed 22 thought bubbles reading "OMIGOD! Lawsuit!") Much more importantly, though, we watched Bob's metaphorical light bulb go off.

The next day I got a call from Verschuren telling me that Bob had sent out a memo to the field asking his folks to replace the unwieldy shopping carts with a more user (read: women)-friendly version. It was fascinating to witness his one-dimensional (male) world view shift to one that more widely acknowledged different realities existed for different people. This happened simply because of a change in the lens he used, one that was gender based.

Verschuren is now embarking on another one of her many firsts as she takes The Home Depot into China. As she explains: "The way I run retail is tight/loose: tight on making the stores safe, productive, and in stock, but loose in terms of giving managers the space to try a new event, new product, and the freedom to fail legitimately. I myself have failed and there have been people there to protect me when I have failed, but it had to be legitimate failure."

Verschuren has demonstrated that her approach to transforming The Home Depot's corporate strategy reflects her own personality. Many would argue that her work on the gender front is a made-and-"stayed"-in-Canada phenomenon, with The Home Depot US lagging behind its Canadian counterpart.

The people on her team are now understanding that their organization has a personality of its own, one that has been greatly affected by the organization's leadership. In order to achieve success, the team members need to support that personality or culture. They have to consider themselves as forward thinking and innovative in order to really fit well within this organization and help it change, adapt, and lead.

Verschuren was able to explain and demonstrate to the other members of the team what is wrong with the current way of doing things. She intuited from her own experience with her family's organic transition that if the people in the chain understood why change is necessary, they may be more motivated to adapt to new methods.

Michéle Andrews, an organizational change expert whom I've often worked with, offers this insight: "Annette's work is worthy of note because she came at change systemically using the gender lens she was passionate about. Frankly, she went well beyond traditional marketing and promotion strategies to reinforce her new business direction. Everything she did— hiring and succession, rewards and recognition, training and development—all were pulled through the gender lens. She had the courage and tenacity to take the long view. Making this kind of fundamental change takes time, and involves looking into every corner of your organization, but the results speak for themselves."

And that, as they say folks, is leadership.

CHAPTER FOUR

Organizational Readiness:
So, Who's Driving This Tractor?

Being prime minister is a lonely job . . . you cannot lead from the crowd.

—Margaret Thatcher, Former British Prime Minister

Boasting about a distinguished farming lineage tends not to be common to most company CEOs that we've met. What is common, however, is that those few leaders that have begun to create a gender-intelligent ecosystem do so with a business model that reflects consumer-based gender differences. These leaders know they need to step back and figure out where they are on the gender-intelligence continuum. (It's helpful to know which direction to drive the tractor.) There is also a fundamental "awareness" that one must fertilize before one plants. In other words, smart leaders think about what needs to be done in order to prepare the company for change.

GETTING THE LAY OF THE LAND
• Start with figuring out your company's current ecosystem: Where are you on the gender-intelligence continuum?
• Ask: What needs to be done in order to properly prepare your internal culture for change?

The goal of this chapter is to help you plant the seed for the transformation of the culture within your company and to prepare everyone—top down, bottom up, and inside out—to develop a new internal ecosystem. It starts with donning a new pair of glasses.

In order for a company to really get this right, a gender-lens strategy needs to take hold within the *core* of the organization. To achieve this, two things need to be in place: (1) people to figure out where the company currently sits in the gender-intelligence continuum, and (2) a team who is willing to drive the organizational tractor in a new direction. Essentially, someone needs to be sitting in the executive boardroom, fully licensed to go anywhere he or she needs to. That's where leadership comes in.

RETAIL'S CHALLENGES IN GOING ORGANIC

Just Who *Is* Minding the Store?

Thinking like an organic farmer requires a special kind of leadership. Herein lies a big part of the problem. Sean, a 15-year retail veteran and leader in his own right, explains: "Because retail offers little else in the way of strengths other than cash flow, it's tough to attract the talent needed to run this pretty complicated business. The usual retail ailments run the gamut of poorly paid management and staff, difficult global logistics, razor-thin margins, constant pressure to change and refresh its offering, dispersed operations that are difficult to align, constant consumer and competitive pressure to drive prices down, and limited barriers for competitors to enter the business. What you have is a business environment that can essentially render you irrelevant overnight."

Retail is still a lot like the "Wild West" of the business world. What's interesting, though, is that women actually notice the leadership challenges within this industry. We are frequently asked this rhetorical question: "Lordy, just who *is* running the store?"

Sean sums up: "So the fastest, largest, and most competitive business sector in the Canadian economy struggles with the lack of smart leadership in the tractor seat. There's a consensus out there that most retail executives are good merchants—very skilled at buying things, but not typically nearly as good at selling them. They live in a world of managing markdown allowances."

Diane Brisebois, president of the Retail Council of Canada, says, "Traditional retail struggles with the problem of public perception that goes all the way back to how parents view it as a career option. It goes with high school career counsellors who are not at all compelled to recommend retail as a career choice. Retailers themselves aren't a lot of help because they don't engage in the process of making retail seen as a respected trade. This is unique to Canada. I don't see this in other similar countries like the UK and the US, both of whom view retail as a legitimate career."

Brisebois is doing her part to shift this perception. She is responsible for bringing to life the first retail management school at Ryerson University, and the Retail Council of Canada has started its own program for retail managers with the help of a wide variety of companies. Brisebois says, "There is finally a realization that increasing the level of retail managerial talent is in everyone's best interest."

It's our view that until retail takes itself seriously, it's going to continually wrestle with taking women seriously. But there are glimmers of hope with people like Brisebois and the Retail Council of Canada working to create management and leadership competencies. There are a few bright lights in the leadership department that are blazing a path, folks we'll hear from throughout the book. However, that said, there is still a great vacuum where retail is deemed to be a transitional career, an attitude that needs to not only change in business schools and the broader business community, but within the profession itself.

The MAWG Syndrome

Another encumbrance to becoming a gender-intelligent retailer is another leadership issue, one we affectionately call the MAWG Syndrome. As mentioned previously, MAWG is an acronym for "middle-aged white guy." Simply put, it's a male world view or one-dimensional lens, one seen in abundance in traditional retail monoculture. Historically and, arguably, today, internal company processes and procedures have been developed through this one-dimensional lens. Not that this should surprise anyone. MAWGs created the North American business-management model, while women created the North American family-management model. The business model that exists today is a direct carry-over from the days when it was men selling primarily to the male breadwinner.

Look at the language of business even today: "Sportspeak" and military analogies abound (the front line/officers of the company), hierarchical structures prevail (top dog wins), and definitions of success (more, better, best) all have their genesis in a male-based view of the world. Reflect on most male-based corporate cultures, the ones that hold meetings at 7:30 a.m. or encourage doing business on golf courses or in the bar after work. Think of airplane and automobile seat design that assumes all passengers are 6'0", Stepford wives–permeated advertising, marketing brimming with speeds and feeds, stats and facts rather than women-relevant benefits. Male-based, male-based, male-based. They are all practising monoculture. It's a self-fulfilling prophecy: One might be bold enough to suggest that there aren't the profits there could be because businesses aren't relevant to women. Everyone is chasing the same dollar. When everyone is chasing the same dollar and not differentiating, they all have to run faster and harder to make money, hence the 7:30 a.m. business meetings that are hard for working mothers (and more and more today, fathers) to get to.

However, being a MAWG in the traditional definition doesn't necessarily equate to being middle-aged, white, or, dare I say, even male. While once a pejorative term meaning "a guy who doesn't get it," it doesn't necessarily pertain just to men anymore. Frankly, there is no shortage of women who fall squarely into that traditional definition of MAWG. It's just plain silly to assume that by virtue of sharing the same chromosomal makeup that women automatically know what women consumers want. While the chances are better that women might "get it," by no means is it a sure thing. Corporate culture and company training often require women to adopt (sometimes quite unconsciously) male-based attitudes in order to survive and progress up the ladder. Think about this: *The women of Bay Street/Wall Street do not usually reflect the women of Main Street.*

However, there is a fascinating trend emerging. There is a significantly growing number of men in management who understand the limitations of a male-based world view. In fact, they've always been around but are more and more feeling less encumbered by the choking conformity of conventional business. The Sean McSweeneys, the Charlie Coffeys of Royal Bank Financial Group, and the Mike Donoghues of Allstate of the world (you'll meet them all) are MAWGs, but by physical definition only. They are the catalysts behind some of the most innovative and important work around gender intelligence that we've witnessed to date.

So, the evolution of the once solely pejorative term "MAWG Syndrome" is not only intriguing, it's quite possibly confusing. In the world today, it now not only includes women (as more and more women punch holes through the glass ceiling), but it also boasts a whole new generation of male business leaders who actually "get it." We can no longer lump just male neanderthals into this category.

It's critical to note that you can't *only* look to the women in your organization. Gender intelligence is not about being a woman. It's not even necessarily about being *for* women. It is about having a holistic view of your business, with gender, both women and men, as a core competency. This is something that one doesn't automatically have by virtue of chromosomes. For leaders of both genders to be successful, they need to understand it's about taking a conscious and strategic gender lens to view all parts of the business.

GENDER INTELLIGENCE REQUIRES "AWARE" LEADERSHIP

One sure thing all businesses require in creating a gender-intelligent ecosystem is what we refer to as "awake" and committed leadership. Over the years, some of the most impressive leadership demonstrated in companies is with the grassroots. If a company is lucky, this phenomenon can actually spread throughout an organization. However, the grassroots still need mandate approval from the higher-ups. Ultimately, senior leadership needs to lead and support changes that must happen at the core of the organization in order to create consistency and sustainability of gender intelligence. The Royal Bank is a great example of this.

In 1996, I met with Charlie Coffey, executive vice president at the Royal Bank, to discuss how the bank could improve its approach to women consumers. I explained the business case for gender intelligence, but one of the many things that hit Coffey was when I told him the field was already 10 steps ahead of head office. There was a huge number of account managers who were reaching out to women entrepreneurs in a variety of ways, from conducting seminars to holding networking events. My advice to him was, "Wake up and catch up."

He agreed. As we mentioned earlier, using our program, the bank launched a comprehensive training initiative with the view to help account managers better meet the needs of women entrepreneurs. One year into it, the bank witnessed a 10 percent increase in market share and a 29 percent increase in customer satisfaction levels among women entrepreneurs with their account managers. This, in an industry that spills blood over gaining one- or two-point market share increases.

It comes down to this: Major change requires a transformation within the core. You can't go halfway or do it peripherally. It's an attitude, one that emanates from the inside. Incremental improvements bring incrementally better results. Big improvements, however painful at the time, bring radically better results.

GETTING READY: POINTS TO PONDER

- Have you done an audit of your company culture and processes using a gender lens?

- Women notice everything. Is your brand experience consistent at every possible point throughout the organization?

(Continued)

- Is there a means to measure women's value in the consumer relationship and integrate it into company processes?

- Are there the financial and organizational resources, policies, and practices necessary to hire and keep women employees for the long run?

- Are the events and organizations you sponsor relevant to women?

- Do your advertising and marketing materials portray women authentically?

Management

- Can management articulate what the company brand specifically means to women and can they communicate this effectively to employees?

- Can management quantify the potential of women consumers in terms of volume, market share, and profit opportunities?

- Is management performance measured and rewarded based on customer satisfaction, sales, and market share, as well as employee satisfaction and leadership practices?

Employees

- Do staff understand and support the corporate strategy behind better meeting the needs of women consumers?

- Are your customer touch points equipped to handle or reflect gender differences in communication and consumer behaviour?

- Do you measure and reward employee behaviour that positively influences customer relationships and that is also consistent with the company's goals of a gender-balanced workplace and customer base?

- Is there a means for taking action against off-strategy behaviour?

(Continued)

- Do you solicit and act on ideas and opinions from all stakeholders—customers and employees—alike?
- Does your sales force mirror the market you serve?

HOLDING UP THE SACRED COWS: DEFINING YOUR COMPANY'S CURRENT ECOSYSTEM

Now would be the time when you need to put on your gender lens to scrutinize all of the company's sacred cows. A gender-intelligent ecosystem requires that you understand your strengths and weaknesses, characteristics, and limitations, and be able to work effectively within the framework of your business. There will always be certain conditions that can't be altered and, most assuredly, there will always be trial and error.

A legitimate question to ask when beginning is: Will this process of developing a gender-intelligent ecosystem be a mere blip on the company radar or will it be a "let the bells ring and the banners fly" kind of shift? Perhaps, as most do, it will land in the continuum of anything and everything in between. Depending on the size and complexity of the organization, this can be a massive cultural experiment or it can be just a matter of incorporating a gender lens in all decisions. This is a cakewalk if you're a small company, say, of five people, because chances are the CEO *is* the corporate communications department, sales department, product developer, and marketer.

Will This Cost Me a Fortune?

Does developing a gender-lens strategy cost more money than what the business is already spending? Or is it a more strategic allocation of resources based on heightened awareness? Will adopting a gender-lens strategy cost a business millions of dollars or is it something that you can do with existing budgets? The short answer is yes. The Royal Bank Financial Group chose to invest considerable money in sponsorships and training. Others adopt a mindset that doesn't cost a dime. Then there are all of the possible permutations in between. But one thing they all have in common is the need to figure out where to start. And you can't do that until you figure out where you are standing. All organizations exist somewhere on a gender-intelligence continuum. Your first step is to find out where you are now in order to know where you have to go.

With the gender-intelligent standard as the goal, there are typically four broad-based categories a company can fall into.

RETAIL ECOSYSTEMS
1. Conventional
2. Evolved conventional
3. Transitional
4. The goal: The gender-intelligent (organic) retail ecosystem

1. The Organic or Gender-Intelligent Retail Ecosystem

The conventional retail ecosystem is typically motivated by profits instead of sustainability. It uses whatever means necessary to drive maximum profits over the short term. It's run by uniform management with uniform world views and uniform strategies about uniform products and services to appeal to customers, who, it would also appear, are also uniform. It's pure monoculture, typically with a unidimensional, male-oriented, one-size-fits-all world view to everything, including product development, market research, sales training, marketing and advertising, and customers.

Providing solutions to customers' problems is about fitting them into the good-better-best style of selling, preferably "the best," in order to maximize the sale. The focus is product-centric rather than customer-centric. It's the Henry Ford approach to retailing: You can have any colour of car you want as long as it's black. This organization treats its product and service offering as a transaction: "We got it, you want it." It does not comprehend the concept of adding value to the customer. If presented with a problem outside of their product or service scope, the typical response is, "Nope, don't sell that." "Nope, don't know where you can get it, either." The folly of this approach is that consumers often feel that they are something that needs to be dealt with versus someone who needs to be understood and listened to. The only solace here is that these organizations are relatively democratic in delivering bad service to both women and men.

Women are not even on the radar as customers or employees. In this conventionally run company culture, women often tend to be at the periphery and generally in the limited roles of administration or cashiers. Even if a few make the hallowed halls of executive row, they will likely be co-opted into working within the male-based culture. This type of company survives at this lower substrate primarily because it possesses either a geographical or unique product advantage. However, this type of retailer can be easily overtaken by any forward-thinking competitor as it tends to survive through a strategy that is price-based.

Who falls into this category? Well, no surprises. Our study revealed that automotive dealers, home-improvement and home-electronic stores, and home builders live very comfortably here. The services sector fared marginally better with women, but overall, scored really, really low. Relatively speaking, banks scored okay with women. Then came phone companies, invest-ment firms, and insurers, with government services bringing up the rear.

CONVENTIONAL RETAILER
• The conventional retail ecosystem operates as a monoculture.
• Such an organization uses "good-better-best" hierarchical retailing.
• The product/service offering is a transaction with a "We got it, you want it" attitude.
• Issues outside of the narrow niche of product or service are all but ignored. It's about selling product, not providing solutions.
• Gender bias is evident with a latent view that women are less knowl-edgeable/capable than men. The company covertly or overtly uses sexist language, humour, and images.
• They have little or no understanding of the physical retail environment as it relates to women's preferences.
• It democratically delivers bad service to both men and women.

There's no point taking up valuable print space by illustrat-ing a conventional retailer. Simply walking out your front door and getting on with the business of your day will bring you face-to-face with any number of them. However, it *is* worthwhile to highlight an example of organic thinking in an industry renowned for conventional retailing practices. Here's a story of an entrepreneur who had a successful business idea that had its genesis from what she calls "that mess in the automotive industry." Karen Jamison utterly rejected all things "conventional" in order to appeal to women consumers. She came out of the gates with an organic business model, separating herself from the industry pack that is drowning in conventional monoculture.

CASE STUDY: CLUTCH

In early 2007, Karen Jamison started Clutch, a car dealership specializing in late-model reselling to women, offering everything from Toyota Corollas to Ferraris. After a successful career in cosmetics marketing, Jamison approached autoOne in BC with the concept of a dealership that would appeal to women. Using her own innate gender lens, the result was Clutch.

Jamison's research found that women were buying 54 percent of new/used vehicles, yet their experience as consumers was very poor. She explains: "The car industry is a really big monolith, run by men for men. Women are treated with the very popular 'Go get your husband' approach to selling cars. Men aren't happy either, but they don't walk away feeling offended like women consumers. They just walk away accepting that the experience didn't fully meet their needs."

Jamison began with the physical environment and created a totally different space, one quite apart from the usual square box, antiseptic car dealership type. It has an art gallery feel, with a long, narrow profile, high ceilings, and art on the walls. The look is contemporary, sexy, and fresh, with attention to details like great lighting and fresh flowers.

While ambience is essential to the overall experience, it wasn't the building that drove women mental. Jamison knew that to appeal to women, the sales experience had to be excellent. The only way to break through the noise, to stop women from hitting that proverbial mute button, was to metaphorically declare, "This ain't business as usual." When women walk into Clutch, Jamison says, "They don't feel like prey in the shark tank. The client is greeted, but is allowed to choose the sales associate they want to deal with. The first part of the transaction is informational. We like to slow the prospective client down as this transaction is, after a house, one of the biggest purchasing decisions people make."

Women are made to feel like they can take all the time in the world (if they want) to make an informed choice. Jamison allows two to three hours for the sales process. But she's only too happy to meet your needs if you want to call up and say, "Find me X car for Y amount and call me back when you have found it." "The experience at Clutch is intimate, personalized," says Jamison. She's also quick to point out that it is not just about the high-end sale. The company took great pride in finding a late-model Corolla for $16,000 versus $23,000 (new) for one particular 73-year-old customer. Not only were they able to save her money, but this grandmother enjoyed a hassle-free car-buying experience, something she says she's never had.

At Clutch, all cars are mechanically inspected and any issues highlighted from the inspection are taken care of. As well,

Clutch completely reconditions the vehicles so that they are cosmetically (inside and out) showroom-ready. Clutch will carry only cars that have spotless ICBC (Insurance Corporation of British Columbia) and Carfax reporting, so owners are guaranteed not to get a lemon. But the company is not limited to pre-owned vehicles. They regularly buy wholesale from the branded dealers on behalf of their clients, saving them time, money, and hassle.

Jamison feels that her business is not just selling cars, it's also (if not even more) about connecting people and creating a community for women. Clutch hosts events such as a fundraiser raffling off a Ferrari for a community group that helps single moms. They sponsored a women's driving program, the first ever that taught women to drive on a real NASCAR track. No one had ever done this before because it had been assumed that women would never go for something like this. Wrong. Women loved it.

In fact, the majority of her business is generated word of mouth from past clients as well as repeat business. The authentic, family-like social atmosphere is what many car companies strive for, but Jamison has successfully achieved it.

Jamison hasn't done anything here that had significant structural costs. Car dealerships are really pretty simple set-ups—big rooms with cars and salespeople. What Jamison has done is change the way her salespeople approach a sale and incented them to make it a good experience for women. What has resulted is, even though the focus is on women, they are now getting a lot of business from men, who also appreciate the gender-intelligent approach that Jamison is taking. (As you will hear us say throughout this book, meet the needs of women and you'll exceed the expectations of men.)

The lesson for other car dealers that Clutch demonstrates is: If you did nothing else but change your *attitude* toward women customers, you could experience similar results. Jamison's success has as much to do with her approach of "How can we do better?" as it does with the nice-to-haves, like the couches and the cappuccino bar. These are important because they signal that there is something very different going on here.

2. The Evolved Conventional Retail Ecosystem

An evolved conventional retail ecosystem has a modicum of either accidental or unconscious gender intelligence or demonstrates an effort to do the right thing regarding women consumers, but, for a variety of reasons, such as size, industry perception, negative media coverage, or inconsistent application of a gender lens, women still experience or perceive the organization as operating within the conventional realm.

There are a lot of service-based companies sequestered in this category, including phone companies, financial institutions, and government services. In an evolved retailer or service provider, company amenities are generally fully developed and the product offering is usually relevant to women, though women have to do the work to find that out for themselves. The work culture has women in influential roles as well as people who understand that women are an important part of the customer base. However, they still run up against the side effects of monoculture, which still proliferates. While there may be gender-based initiatives undertaken in an attempt to turn the company around, the tractor is driven by instinct rather than knowledge. Unfortunately, this lack of a strategic approach is intuited quickly by women. It's that whole "fem-marketing" rat thing.

In the evolved conventional category, you'll also often find a champion who will try to run up against the establishment. They meet with varying degrees of success but the monolith is just too large, too entrenched for them to bring about appreciable differences. But that doesn't stop certain people from trying to make a dent.

Government is an interesting example of an organization needing to "cut through the noise." It's testosterone-laden and about as neanderthal as it is possible to get, certainly from most women's perspectives. It's also a complex animal. You need to specialize in metaphorical fist-fighting and not-so-metaphorical sarcastic humour and yelling if you are going to survive in government. The ratio of women to men almost guarantees that the women in the room either have to be "pound-on-the-desk radicals/tough broads" to get heard or they don't get a voice. In government, the women's caucus tends to carry "baggage" as they are often viewed as whiners and advocates of "soft issues." This makes it very hard to compete for the floor. Then, of course, there's connecting with women constituents, not only at election time, but every day when it comes to delivering services.

Needless to say, no one was more surprised than I was when I picked up a phone message one day in 2006. The caller simply said, "Hello, Joanne. My name is Gordon Campbell. I'm the premier of British Columbia. I've just finished your book and

I'm interested in chatting with you about how to take some of these ideas and make it work with my team. Give me a call when you have a moment." I shook my head ruefully, mentally going through the names of the dozen or so wiseacres I know who might have thought a prank like this was funny. But the message was legit. I met the premier the following week.

Premier Campbell was very aware of the need to connect better with women in the civil service and women constituents. He was interested in knowing how his government could "speak the same language" as women about issues they cared about. This was just as important from an internal employee perspective, since the majority of public servants are women. Said Campbell, "In my view, women are an invaluable resource since they are strong stakeholders in public opinion and government policy making and consumer decision making."

He was also cautious in his approach to leading the way for change. He had to ensure buy-in from caucus members and deputy ministers. As an elected official, he could direct, not mandate, which made things, well, political. The questions came fast and furious: How do you get women constituents engaged? How do we communicate the full context of an issue in a relevant way so women will hear what we are trying to say? Is it possible to measure progress and how do you reward good performance against a plan? Are there visible, low-hanging fruit or easy-to-implement initiatives that will make an impact? Where do people go for knowledge?

His enthusiasm was noteworthy, but there was no way the premier was going to be able to move this *Queen Mary* around in his own lifetime—let alone by the end of his tenure—and he recognized this. He needed to conduct gender-based research and polls and figure out how to connect with communities of women. Gender differences in communication styles needed to be factored into meeting protocols to make sure everyone was being heard. In fact, a complete gender-based audit was needed on all public communications, policies, processes, and practices, looking at potential barriers to women.

While this list was daunting, what *was* helpful was the premier's own innate gender lens. That was half the battle.

We addressed the premier's desire to educate his cabinet, caucus, and deputy ministers in a series of sessions focusing on what corporate North America was doing around gender. Campbell rightfully wanted to lead by example rather than have us tell them what to do. The responses to the sessions on gender intelligence ran the gamut of wholly supportive to those scared off by the "feminist agenda."

But that didn't stop the premier in his own sphere of influence. He used gender intelligence in all he could personally touch and affect. He created a women's caucus (though many in the women's caucus would argue it wasn't taken at all seriously by most of the other members of government). A guideline was created for policy makers called *Best Practices in Gender Analysis*, which helped zero in on policy development using a gender lens. Campbell admitted that this particular initiative, while pretty controversial within his government, was very much needed. *The Convention on the Elimination of All Forms of Discrimination against Women (CEDAW)*, adopted in 1979 by the UN General Assembly, is often described as an international bill of rights for women. Consisting of a preamble and 30 articles, it defines what constitutes discrimination against women and sets up an agenda for national action to end such discrimination. In 2003, the BC government was criticized by CEDAW for its economic policies. The province's budget cuts were having a disproportionately negative effect on women. This is a classic example of why a gender lens is essential.

Campbell wanted to speak directly with women constituents and did so through focus groups. He explains: "Part of our effort is to put the government in a position where we hear women's voices from a broad range of backgrounds. To that end, we have supported programs that encourage participation of women in small businesses, as well as in non-traditional industries like construction and mining. We have hosted the Congress on Women's Safety, the Aboriginal Women's Dialogue and the Dialogue on Women."

Campbell makes sure there is a critical mass of women in key leadership positions. He says, "It is through having women in positions of importance that we will help shape public responses. Women are playing an increasingly important role in assuring that our work ethic engages our workforce in facing the challenges and opportunities created by work within the public service."

Today, 48.9 percent of the management positions in BC's public service are held by women, compared to 28.5 percent in 1990. Says Campbell, "Women make a major contribution to this government, both in developing our agenda and in implementing it. The deputy premier and minister of finance, the deputy minister to the premier and the deputies of environment, citizens' services, and the associate deputy of housing play crucial roles in shaping the critical cornerstones of our foundation for action."

Not afraid to step ahead of the pack, Campbell is working toward creating a gender-based perspective throughout the government. Like many leaders, his style is to mould his personal vision into how the government operates, both at a macro and micro level. His government's recent highly heralded work on the environment file is a strong testament to how leadership can make a difference in controversial, complex areas. Campbell is the first to admit the distance yet to travel is considerable. But as Sean muttered one day, "At least he's put the key in the tractor and turned the bloody thing on."

EVOLVED CONVENTIONAL RETAILER

- For the evolved conventional retailer, initiatives are more accidental/ instinctual than strategic.

- Parts of gender intelligence are present, but it's not yet a core competency.

- The retailer exhibits a desire to be different, but may not know how to start.

- Champions for gender intelligence exist but in isolated pockets and are not necessarily formally recognized.

- Women may be in positions of influence, but are not necessarily gender intelligent.

- The business case around women consumers is marginally understood, but the company still operates primarily in the conventional realm.

- Women/men consumers still perceive or experience the company as a monoculture—one size fits all.

The next two levels of retail ecosystems make up the very heart of this book. In fact, it's where most companies are or will end up if they take the advice in these pages. The case studies used to illustrate these two ecosystems, Allstate Canada and Mountain Equipment Co-op, are so powerful that they each warrant a chapter of their very own.

3. The Transitional Retail Ecosystem

Retailers who have decided to transition to a gender-intelligent retail ecosystem have begun to assume full responsibility for implementing a gender lens in all of their practices and procedures. A company that is planning to transition to gender-intelligent ecological principles knows its fundamental business practices are sound and organized, but knows that by becoming gender intelligent, they will only get better. They have a good management system in place, and an ability to communicate, train their staff, and manage a change process. You aren't likely to find this in a monoculture and, consequently, the transition is not likely to be executed well.

The transitional retail ecosystem has leadership energy supporting it from above and below and is prepared to be flexible and adaptable. There is usually an internal champion guiding the company to this point, one that has been formally mandated. This person often uses opportunities that have low capital costs to demonstrate the benefits of gender intelligence to the organization. This generally means changes to areas that are procedural versus those that fall under capital costs. They look for places where they can pilot ideas that will have measurable and demonstrable results that will show the organization the success of these initiatives. They start small but plan big. The next chapter will clearly illustrate this.

TRANSITIONAL RETAILER

- The transitional retailer clearly defines organizational values (like diversity) that align with gender intelligence.

- The company demonstrates flexibility and adaptability to changing/transitioning.

- The organization develops a learning culture, creating an environment that is filled with people who love to learn new skills.

- Leadership is recognized to come from above, as well as from middle management and/or grassroots.

- Internal champions are mandated to help guide the transition.

- The culture supports a process of test/try, fail, adjust, and retry.

- The company looks for early wins/low-hanging fruit.

- The retailer provides venues for women consumers to voice their opinions about products and services.

---

4. The Goal: Organic or Gender-Intelligent Retail Ecosystem

This is a company that has evolved enough that diversity is intrinsic to everything it does. There is strong representation of women decision makers throughout the hierarchy of the organization. This awareness is translated to women consumers by the sophisticated use of language and images that reveal that the company actually understands how women see themselves and the world around them. How women receive and process information and make decisions is integrated into the business model. The company also has a strong corporate social responsibility orientation to their business (corporate soul). Metrics, rewards, and recognition systems clearly reinforce the strategy. In other words, the company creates an experience that *intelligently* recognizes gender differences.

The chart below highlights some of the key characteristics of a gender-intelligent retail ecosystem. Much more on this in Chapter 10.

ORGANIC OR GENDER-INTELLIGENT RETAILER
• In a gender-intelligent retailer, the company leadership aligns overall business strategy with corporate culture and business practices by ensuring there are policies to actually support organizational change.
• A gender lens is applied to all decisions, including strategy and product development, store/office design, sales training, and market research.
• The company focuses on relationships and retention versus one-time transactions.
• Company processes reflect the way both women and men make decisions and process information.
• There is strong representation of women throughout the hierarchy who make decisions and actually sign cheques.
• The organization shows strong social responsibility (corporate soul).
• The retailer recognizes that a superior service experience starts before a woman enters the front door.
• It seeks to create a physical environment that reflects women's needs.
• Products and services are offered through a number of channels: bricks, clicks, and phone.

(Continued)

- The culture demonstrates a sophisticated use of language and images that reflect how women see themselves and the world.

- The company continually looks for ways to engage in a two-way *dialogue* with women.

- Sales force and marketing are not afraid to have/use a sense of humour and playfulness.

- The organization consistently links product features to benefits in a way that is relevant to women.

- Customer points of contact demonstrate excellent social skills.

- Staff have some authority to solve problems and create solutions with minimal supervision.

- Communications provide *relevant* information that helps women make informed decisions.

This is an ambitious list, and one worthy of aspiration. In Chapter 10, we will profile a company that comes as close to this standard as anyone could today—Mountain Equipment Co-op. This is precisely the reason I seconded poor Sean away from his current life and threw him into the role of writer. At the time of writing, he is still speaking to me.

COMMON GENDER-INTELLIGENT LEADERSHIP THEMES

What do Annette Verschuren, Charlie Coffey, Gordon Campbell, and Karen Jamison all have in common?

- They were in positions of significant influence in their organizations, however large or small.

- They were able to see that understanding women was more than a shift in marketing strategy. Sustainable change had to be much more fundamental, requiring much broader thinking, to bring about the results they were after.
- Their own credibility as leaders was enhanced by the "walk the talk" approach they took to making these changes.
- They all demonstrated having a clear vision, tenacity, and courage to take their organizations in new directions, making some tough decisions along the way. They knew it was a long-term approach, and their perseverance certainly paid off.

YOU'RE KIDDING! CAR INSURANCE?

Property and casualty insurance does not exactly conjure up images of happy women customers cavorting about, singing company accolades. Nor is it something you necessarily equate with cutting-edge leadership. If ever there was an example of a company historically mired in traditional monoculture (the place was run for years by former marines, for heaven's sake!), this is it. Meet Christianne Dostie and Mike Donoghue, two inspiring examples of leaders who are on their way to achieving great results. This is a Pygmalion story if ever there was one. Allstate Canada, a classic example of a transitional retailer, is going organic.

CHAPTER FIVE

Allstate Transitions to Organic

If women didn't exist, all the money in the world would have no meaning.

—Aristotle Onassis, Shipping Magnate

We begin by giving a nod to Christianne Dostie. As Allstate's VP of strategic planning, she and company CEO Mike Donoghue have overturned traditional thinking about how insurance is bought and sold. Donoghue has an unparalleled sense of the big picture and a mind so open you could drive a truck through it. As we speak, this formidable team is working through an enormous corporate transition that puts "relationship" at the epicentre of the strategic-planning process.

Mike Donoghue describes the company's growth philosophy: "We've actually come at this organically. Other big companies in the P&C industry who have grown in Canada have used the traditional mergers-and-acquisition route to double-digit growth. There are over 200 players, so getting one point growth in market share was a challenge. Most companies, including the top 20, average a share between 2 percent to 7 percent of the market, and those who do top 7 percent sure haven't done it organically. We rolled around in this malaise and have been at 2 percent market share forever."

Allstate Canada's massive strategic repositioning and resulting culture change actually had its genesis in the 1980s and early

1990s. Donoghue explains: "Our history was that we either grew our business and didn't make any money, or we made money and didn't grow our business. We weren't able to pull both levers at the same time. I was worried and I needed to create a sense of urgency that if we wanted a future, we needed to fix this. So we fought fires for a couple of years and fixed our bottom line. This allowed us to start talking about strategic planning. That's what got us to the place where we recognized we needed a new vision and mission." Enter Christianne Dostie.

Dostie smiles as she relates her take. "We needed to break out of our roller-coaster cycle. I knew women were going to be intrinsic to this with our new relationship focus. But first I needed to establish the business case around becoming a gender-intelligent company as a way to sustainably shift the company culture."

The Canadian arm of Allstate created an entirely new business model, one that affected the whole organization in order to more consistently serve customers' needs. Donoghue explains: "We landed on the relationship model because the landscape is changing." Naturally, the prize Dostie and Donoghue had their eye on was the organic standard, but, from a gender-intelligence perspective, Allstate was definitely conventional. It was clear to Dostie that the needle had to move. She says, "I believe relationship is a great differentiator in the retail and services business because, unlike products and price, it cannot be copied and pasted. This is a competitive advantage and a long-lasting one, and that's why I wanted to bring women into the strategic conversation in a meaningful way. Women are all about relationships, building networks, and referring friends and family. If you understand how they think, how they buy, and how they refer, well, I'm telling you, it's a brilliant place for a company to take seriously and explore as they undertake a strategic transformation."

Her challenge, or as Dostie aptly puts it, her "opportunity," was to convince senior management to at least look at women consumers from a business opportunity point of view. She relates that her positioning was simply this: "We do a lot of work to understand the cultural differences. Why wouldn't we want to understand 52 percent of the market? I also knew we had to ask ourselves some pretty tough questions. Was Allstate willing to hold up all of our sacred cows and face them dead on?"

Dostie's personal gender lens was sharp with her own experiences leaping into the fray. She explains: "As a consumer, I'm not treated the way I should be. I have to bring my husband along when I buy certain things. I also visit our agencies, so I know that the customer service we are providing is not exactly women friendly. Our sales force is not representative of the total population, though I have to say I'm very proud of our multicultural representation. It's actually not so much about what we're doing; it's much more about what we're *not* doing." She was not without reservation, though, and not for the reasons you might think.

A WOMAN'S PLACE . . . ?

Like many women executives, Dostie was concerned about being the flag-bearer for gender-related issues within the company. She knew all too well the history and perception of women who lobbied on the platform of gender. They are viewed very differently than men advocating the same thing. Dostie recalls her thoughts: "How could I bring this to the table being a woman? You're seen as pushy when you say, 'Hey, guys, we need to focus on women.'"

She worried that it wouldn't be taken as seriously as it would be if it were a man introducing the idea. So, to begin the internal sales pitch, she teamed up with Michael Kaye, a consultant. Kaye would bring the topic of gender to the table, but then Dostie would take over. She describes her approach: "I was a woman talking to a bunch of men, so to catch the guys' attention, I came at it talking their language—financial performance. This was also my language, so I was pretty comfortable with it."

When I mentioned to Donoghue Dostie's concern about being a woman doing this work, he was a bit taken aback, but he was also astute enough to realize that this wouldn't have even crossed his radar as a male executive. He says, "It's very likely that my workplace reality as a man is different from hers." He goes on to explain: "We have a tendency to pay attention to talented people and Christianne earned the respect of the leadership team. We've seen her work, and there's much more to her than hyperbole or gender-speak. She was able to establish a base of credibility for the gender work, which would not likely have survived if she was *just* promoting feminism within the organization. She was very clear she wanted to operationalize gender intelligence throughout the organization, but didn't give us a piece of paper that says, 'Here are the ABCs of gender intelligence.' It was much more intrinsic than that. With Christianne's guidance, we now answer to what we call 'principles' that affect how we do business right across the board."

DEFINING ALLSTATE'S CURRENT ECOSYSTEM

The executive team at Allstate needed to figure out where they currently stood. Donoghue says, "We weren't delivering a consistent level of service. Our internal research revealed that only

48 percent of our customers got a renewal contact call. We needed to make this happen with more consistency. That's where the gender-lens piece came in."

As we speak, this innovative company is operationalizing gender intelligence throughout the organization. Donoghue explains: "What was challenging (and continues to be) to our business folks here is the faith required to make 'relationship' and 'customer experience' a full-blown business concept. Relationships are hard to measure and tie directly back to a sale. How do we measure returns on faith/values–based systems? These are the types of things that challenge our employees to take the leap to embedding gender-based approaches into our sales, product, and systems processes."

Our organizational change guru, Michéle Andrews, says Allstate's situation is an example of a leader sensing the organization is change-ready. "There's generally some kind of a business imperative that will drive the change. The demographics are changing, the competition is heating up, or growth is stagnant. It's usually not a question of 'Is the organization ready to change?' It's more about 'Can the organization survive if it doesn't?' Beyond that, the lament for the leaders in the company then becomes 'Where exactly are we now and how do I get this place ready for change?'"

CONVERTING THE SKEPTICS

Dostie took many steps toward converting the organization's skeptics in the drive to transform Allstate into a gender-intelligent retailer. One huge barrier was the strongly held belief that women weren't involved or interested in property and casualty insurance decisions, and that this was an area most often delegated to men.

Dostie had the unenviable task of trying to sell the concept of reaching out to a constituency that many in the industry felt didn't carry much weight in the decision-making process or even represent enough independent volume to worry about paying attention to in a meaningful way. This is where we came in.

Our company conducted market research to find out how involved women were in the purchasing process. As we all, including Dostie, had anticipated, the results showed that women weren't only involved, they were the *primary* influencers and, in most situations, the family decision makers regarding property and casualty insurance. Though women may not necessarily be the ones talking to the agents, they are the ones pulling the strings behind the scene. When Dostie shared these results with Donoghue, he sat up very straight in his chair.

Donoghue describes the origin of the fallacy that women weren't involved in insurance decision making. "I was actually part of the group that didn't believe women made the decisions . . . At the time I had 10 people on my senior executive team: two were women, eight were men. We went around the room and all the men said, 'I'm the one who makes those decisions . . . ' It didn't occur to me at the time they were making the decisions because they were *in* the industry. We took things for granted. We hadn't asked ourselves the right questions in a while and Dostie helped us to do that.

"The other reason we were slow to operationalize the purchasing power of women was because our fundamental operations were built during a time in history that predates the societal changes that brought women into the economic sphere of influence. Immediately following the postwar period, many companies, ours included, were run by senior executives who came out of the military culture. Allstate Corporation had a number of ex-marines at the helm, which, incidentally, led the company to its dominant position today. In fact, being a marine was a badge of honour at that time. So now we're into the sixties and we needed to respond to changes in society."

Donoghue continues: "The men in charge had a macho culture. They hired other men. Why? Tradition. We hire what we know. Talented women didn't necessarily have their eye on our industry. Male 'car culture.' Probably a combination of the above. Even today women encounter this bias when they buy a car. Our company, me included, had to change, and we did on a number of fronts. Women did enter our workplace and we responded to the 'glass ceiling' debates and affirmative action. In fact, Allstate Corporation has won *Working Mother* magazine's recognition for the past 14 years in a row as a great company for working moms. This did not happen by accident, but it takes time to change fundamental operations and the mindsets that built them. There can be skeptics in the crowd. And sometimes, we still can miss the obvious—the fact that women have incomes, women do research on things, women buy important things, and they do it in a manner that is different from the way our systems and processes have been set up to sell to them. And it costs money to change, so the payoff had better be seen to be worth the effort to change what history and time has already built."

Indeed, Donoghue is a shining example of the power of the converted skeptic. Sean and I have discovered first-hand the important role this corporate skeptic subculture, which exists in all companies, can play. The first task in doing so is understanding *precisely* what it is that people are skeptical about. It often sounds something like "That may be the case for company X, but not here . . . ,"

"There's no difference between women and men . . . ," "The women in *this* company don't feel this way, we've asked them . . . ," or, in Allstate's case, "Men make the decisions, . . ." You simply can't move forward until you intelligently deal with these barriers. Here are a couple of ways that Dostie used to approach this issue. They were very successful in swaying her company's skeptic subculture.

CREATIVELY USE BEST PRACTICES

Dostie demonstrated how gender intelligence worked in other companies, something we call "best practice." Both she and Kaye invited company board members to a session, asking them to come prepared with a brand-positioning strategy that they had previously successfully implemented. One board member had worked for Canadian Tire, so he talked about the company's initiatives to capture women customers and wallet share. Much to Dostie's delight, he commented, "Even though the man is pushing the cart, it's the woman that decides what goes into it." Dostie laughs, "With that story of how Canadian Tire started to realign itself, our job to put women consumers on the table became easier."

This was a critical process for the organization because of the internal awareness that it generated. As Dostie describes it, "Once you create an impetus for awareness, people wake up to what's happening all around them . . . But we knew we still had to bring the executives up the education curve."

LIVE IN THE CUSTOMER'S HIGH-HEELED SHOES

It is crucial that everyone work as a team in order to achieve gender intelligence as a companywide, integrated core competency. Dostie also understood that managers needed not only to learn gender intelligence but to communicate and coach it to others. We conducted a day-long session for executives from product development, operations, sales, human resources, communications, marketing, advertising, and customer service. One of the goals was to get people to understand women's consumer DNA, which required a conscious rather than an instinctual approach to understanding and connecting with women consumers. By the end of the day, people finally internalized that women make the majority of the consumer decisions, yet continue to feel they aren't taken as seriously as men. Participants began to develop their own internal gender lens. Dostie's own approach to encouraging new thinking was participatory, highly visual, consultative, and engaging. Her seminars were rarely lectures, but objective lessons in self-examination. Her work was successful because the outcomes and resulting opinions were always "owned" by the individuals and therefore by the group.

But the truth remains that you can *tell* people anything you want, but if adopting a gender lens is actually going to change behaviour, it needs to mesh with their own values and company reality, and they must be able to relate it to their own experience in some way. While we gave Allstate folks a gender lens, it had to be coupled with their corporate culture, job responsibilities, priorities, and budgets. It was important that everyone recognize and agree upon what would prompt change quickly and also figure out the lagging areas that would hamper efforts.

Dostie described the effect. "This executive session was when the penny dropped for the group. The desire to build a foundation was created. They saw there was definitely a business opportunity in reaching out to women consumers."

Michéle Andrews adds: "There are two things needed to start the chemical reaction of organizational change. As Mike Donoghue and Christianne Dostie demonstrated, change needs to start with the leadership team. A good team includes people who are open to learning what they don't know from the change agents in the field and in middle management. These are the folks closest to the customer.

The front line and line management can be a valuable resource in helping the executive team experience what the consumer is living. The process of stepping into women consumers' shoes needs to be as real as possible. People also need to feel that any initiative undertaken will show results. It's key to provide early, quick wins, the low-hanging fruit, as it were. Pick it, harvest it, and really make it visible so leaders can connect the dots for people. It's important to measure and communicate the results so people can feel some momentum. It lends greater credibility to the efforts, generates confidence in the leaders who are engineering these changes, and swings the skeptics." In today's world, this is more important than ever before. If CEOs don't manage shareholder payouts, they tend to get booted out of the company. We are seeing historically high turnover rates of CEOs and, unfortunately, it appears many are kicked out before they can see the effect of any long-term changes they have put in place. Quick wins and low-hanging fruit will contribute something to short-term profit goals, with the promise of a bigger windfall if the company can stick with the strategy. But if the CEO can't deliver short-term profits or convince shareholders they are worth waiting for, a gender-lens strategy is unlikely to survive—a delicate balancing act, indeed.

With a clear picture of the company's current ecosystem and where the company needed to head, she began by focusing the lens on the company's so-called PESTs. She had to figure out how to change from a very traditional monoculture to one that cultivated gender-intelligent *P*roducts, sales *E*nvironment, *S*elling and communication tools, and *T*raining for customer points of contact. In other words, it was time to operationalize gender intelligence.

OPERATIONALIZING GENDER INTELLIGENCE

Product

One of Allstate's first quandaries was figuring out how they could make themselves unique in an industry where everyone sells government-mandated automobile products. Part of the challenge was differentiating Allstate when the market had trained consumers to shop for insurance products on price.

The questions were simple: What will be our positioning in the marketplace? How can we differentiate ourselves from the competitors when *everybody's* talking about customer service and building relationships and essentially sells the same products?

Product = Peace of Mind

Allstate's public relations manager, Karyn Toon, explains the thinking: "Relationship, whether at the time of claims settlement or at new business writing, offers a series of value-laden processes as one way of talking about our 'product'—things like 'Know me,' 'Respect me,' 'Make it simple for me.' There are huge systems implications to each of these deliverables at the time of creating product or processes to make sure we know who we are talking with and what they deem of value to buy. The assumption is that relationship is worth paying for, something we know women value, especially when I can get the same product everywhere else. This resulted in an over-riding brand positioning called 'Your Choice,' insurance on our customers' terms. Relevant choice is a critical concept to women, as is having their preferences acknowledged and op-tions provided from which they can choose. By January 2008 every market had a product called 'Your Choice Home,' a base homeowner product that allowed customers to choose from a selection of optional features and benefits such as 'Yard and Garden' packages or 'Student Protection' packages. Further product options under the Choice umbrella will follow on the auto side as well."

Environment

In order to help Allstate determine the weak links, our company conducted a comprehensive, gender-based mystery visit program in the field that evaluated everything from the office environment through to and including customer follow-up. The mystery visits did reveal breakdowns in the overall customer experience, whether you were man, woman, or child.

Often there was a lack of a formal reception area and a lack of privacy. Many times we walked right into an agent's personal space, offices were messy, or there was no place to leave your coat. Sean, as my spouse, received much more business-focused attention than I did. There was a lack of consistent corporate branding and so on.

The company heard from us loud and clear that women's consumer experience involves so much more than just the direct retail transaction. And while the goal was to improve the overall customer experience, Dostie and her team focused specifically on what women experienced, knowing it would raise the bar for everyone. The report not only highlighted what happened during the sales process, but included descriptions of parking, lighting, landscaping, the directional signage, and the building itself, including washrooms, seating, the amount of natural light, and so on. These areas are usually seen as a financial drain on a company, but in reality, they are assets as they provide a supporting role in the transaction for consumers, especially women. These amenities act as a barometer of an organization's gender intelligence. Dostie and Donoghue recognized that the management teams in gender-intelligent organizations are directed and resourced so that they can make these a part of their priorities. In fact, they came to understand these issues to be *as* important as other priorities in their business.

A big transition for the company was moving from 250 locations to 103 larger retailers, bigger and more visible, and relocating to where people are. There were many upsides to reducing office locations. Donoghue explains: "We are now fully funding the distribution system versus asking agents to share in that funding as was done previously. This allows the agents to focus on their areas of expertise, such as sales and relationship development, rather than have them focus on recruiting and training, which were not their strengths. We'll do that because we're good at that. As a result of our specialized nature, we'll be able to ensure that our processes, whether they are service or sales processes, are more consistent. You could try to manage these things from afar, but when you have 300 locations, it makes the job more difficult than if you have 100 locations, not that 100 is going to be easy either."

The offices themselves received the gender-lens treatment. Dostie says, "Our new office design is reflecting what we've discovered through the research and the mystery visits. There's actually an aesthetic now, wonderful lighting, trendy colours, a kids' play area, among many other things. The research also revealed that women respond to environmental positioning more than men do, so we have moved to an environmentally friendly, made-in-Canada approach."

But Allstate's environment approach goes further than pure aesthetics. Donoghue describes it this way: "The newly designed offices have the manager up front, so he or she can specifically come and say hello. This, to me, is the gender lens. It speaks more to establishing that important relationship. It's not about transaction. We're done with that. If it's a transaction we wanted, we'd go direct or have a call centre."

Sales Tools

Marketing and Advertising

Donoghue says, "The key messages for our company are protection, safety, knowledge, respect, and transparency. From a gender-lens perspective, we know these are things high up on a priority list. You get to these things through consistency and a level-handedness that makes it clear you have nothing to hide and trustworthy expertise to share." Toon adds: "For example, insurance advertising is traditionally fairly heavy-handed, overly serious, and often fear-based: 'You'd better insure yourself or when your house burns down, you'll be left alone, scared, and without resources.' The gender-based research told us that fear does not resonate well with women consumers as a tactic to influence purchase. Our first real ad campaign incorporating gender concepts was around identity theft. We worked very hard to get campaign imagery and slogans that incorporated humour without being flippant. It's a fine balance because at the end of the day, we also must be perceived as stable, knowledgeable, and reliable. We continue to redo materials and focus on consistency, clarity, white space, simple explanations, light-handed approaches to colour, and imagery . . . These are gender concepts, but they are also good branding strategies in general."

The Web

Allstate's internal research revealed that people who check out the company online ultimately buy from them, but not necessarily via the online process. When they don't buy online, they walk into an agency. It was compelling information—people explore and get information online, but the purchase is made through an individual. This had "women" written all over it. Allstate's executive team recognized the crucial role of the Internet in the sales process. They have worked to ensure there is consistency and clarity on their website. They have added information-laden sound bites and have made sure information on the company's work in the community was available on the home page. Allstate has also added material to make consumer rights and privacy more apparent. In terms of making life simpler, which is an important consideration for women, they have made the most important information the most prominent and easiest to find and have simplified the quote-and-buy process so it takes less time—20 minutes instead of 45.

Knowing women are avid consumers of information and advice, marketing collateral and the website became more educationally focused. As Donoghue explains, "Guys care about this too, but women care more."

The Brand

The Allstate's hands logo with the motto "You're in good hands with Allstate" tested extremely well with women. Donoghue says, "The end stake is for people to see what we're calling the Beacon, the Allstate Hands, a similar strategy with the icon created by the Starbucks and Apple logos."

Training

Our mystery shops revealed that the current customer experience with most of Allstate's field force was purely transactional. There were dazzling exceptions, with a few agents providing an exceptional sales experience. In those situations, when Sean and I masqueraded as husband and wife, we were spoken to with equal attention. The quote was in both of our names or, at the very least, they asked whose name it should be in. Complicated policy jargon was translated and explained in a relevant way. Unfortunately, this was a rarity and not consistent by a long shot. It was pretty evident to us that things had to change in a big way.

Start at the Beginning

We did a gender-based audit on sales training material to ensure that women's world view was represented. We steered scripts away from status-based statements like, "Allstate is the biggest and the best" and incorporated more relationship-style language that articulated relevant lifestyle benefits. The new training approach builds on the relationship dimension rather than a product-focused approach or something that simply enables transactions. Some of the changes are small and subtle, such as training on the importance of the greeting before offering to provide a quote. Other topics covered in training are about better ways to use phone systems to support rather than deflect the relationship. It takes time, however, for people to use the same tools but use them differently than they have been using them for the past 30 years. The training is just the beginning of the culture change process, but critical to supporting it.

Reward the Right Behaviour

Company leadership tackled organization design and hierarchy, role reviews and alignment, and compensation structure, in particular that of their agents. In fact, the remodelling of the distribution system (agents, Internet, and customer contact centres), while necessary for competitive reasons, offered the opportunity to redesign compensation and rewards to better meet the relationship strategies so central to gender intelligence.

Insurance sales traditionally rewards on renewal and new business, and on individual achievements. The new systems still drive desired outcomes for growth and profit, but there are now team compensation systems for overall sales, customer retention, and service. This is probably one of the hardest parts of the transformation to design and implement. It's an incredibly sensitive area of culture change and it takes tremendous commitment on behalf of leadership, management, and employees to understand and embrace the change.

According to Andrews, "Compensation structures and measuring results are often a forgotten set of drivers that are needed to change the behaviour necessary in creating a culture shift. It's the age-old question 'How do I develop the consistency required to maintain this change in culture in the face of high turnover?' Store, branch, or agency managers need to know in very simple terms what the organization is trying to do, what the direction of the organization is, and how, in very practical terms, it can manifest itself at the consumer level. Most importantly, they want to know 'What's in it for me?' But you also need to be measuring the right thing. Many companies try to implement change, but keep traditional scorecards intact, forgetting that old measures drive old behaviours and create real barriers to changing from the status quo. Understanding what results to track and report, to drive the new desired behaviour, is pretty important."

Change Management

The leaders anticipated a strong reaction and they got it. Thankfully, they planned for it. Donoghue says, "Everyone heard about changes at a high level and each of them got a personal letter that talked about the changes more specifically for them individually. On announcement day, every employee had a meeting across Canada in a planned and orchestrated national process that incorporated all media: face-to-face, pre-recorded DVDs of leadership telling the 'why,' carefully trained sales management presentations, all done in front of employees simultaneously in all time zones. Then each agent was spoken to in a one-on-one meeting in sessions that took seven weeks."

Donoghue recalls: "But the problem was if you were in Week Seven, you were still having a lot of angst because we didn't get to you in Week One. I still don't know if we could have done it any differently, just because of the sheer number of people. We could have had meetings with 100 people, but that wouldn't have been as effective. We really talked to people in these meetings about why this whole process was necessary. There was no doubt in my mind that this was one of our big successes. People left agreeing that we needed to make changes. They see where we're going because of the threats from the marketplace. These realities will not allow us to continue the way we were."

Donoghue smiles ruefully. "Out of all the changes we made, changing compensation has been among the most challenging, but we're not throwing people into this. We're doing this over the course of about two years. The bottom line is we're paying people differently—competitively for similar roles, but differently—and this is understandably hard for some of our people. It becomes a lightning rod for overall issues around changing the things that we have to do every day when we come into the office to keep our customers satisfied and remain competitive. It's hard to accept that the things that may have made us successful to this point are not the things that will sustain that success for the long term. We know that some will never accept this, and will move on. Others will adapt and thrive with us."

Andrews adds, "The kinds of compensation changes Allstate is making takes real courage and vision. The changes will be tough, but all the efforts in making change would likely have been futile if they had not taken this step."

Reinforce, Reinforce, Reinforce

Our experience shows that the companies that are the most successful at re-creating their ecosystems are the ones that publicly reinforce the mandate at every opportunity. Dostie says, "Naturally I talk it up all of the time, at every meeting. This new world order is constantly reinforced in all communications. We believe we can't say it enough." Donoghue adds, "If people don't get it the first time, you have to say it again. And if they don't get it the second time, you say it again. And then it has to show up somehow."

Andrews weighs in: "When change comes truly from the inside out and when it's the core leaders who are driving the change, rightly or wrongly, the leaders' level of commitment to the change will be transparent to the rest of the organization. It's a complete waste of resources, money, and time to go out and train sales associates to be relationship-focused and gender-intelligent and not have those beliefs reinforced every time they meet the leadership in words and in action. Employees easily pick up whether or not leaders have put their money where their mouth is and have really made those value-based changes deep in the organization. Employees figure this out in a heartbeat and judge the organization's commitment or project's credibility on this. It is about starting at the top or the bottom, depending upon how you want to talk about the organization, but it's the leadership who needs to change first. The way to change is to enlighten existing leadership, remove encumbrances if they exist, and hire people willing to embrace and lead change."

Author Catherine Aird once said, "If you can't be a good example, then you'll just have to be a horrible warning." She's right.

If the gender lens is being applied at the core of the organization—things like an office or store redesign, compensation and promotion program, or a store's merchandising strategy—and the front-line staff are experiencing the benefit of these tools, systems, and processes, you'll get the change you desire. It's closing the loop and making sure all of the players are connected—the product development people talk to the marketing department, which drives all the promotions; the marketing department talks to the corporate communications department to be sure the gender lens is reflected in internal newsletters and on the website.

Dostie says, "You also need your president on board to begin the necessary cultural shift. I used to be an idealist, but I'm over that now." She explains: "I thought that I could drive transformation bottom up. It won't happen. You will drive some transformation, but not the whole thing. This is why I went into strategic planning. It was the only way that I could influence and get the organization to transform. You also need a company champion, a role I specifically created for myself."

It's also important to remember that you do want a positive culture change to outlast any one champion, but culture change is a double-edged sword. If you think of how hard it is to change corporate culture, you realize it is because it is bigger than any one person, outlasting even the most charismatic of leaders and change agents. In a high-turnover organization, new employees adopt the mindset of the people who are training them and the people they are sitting beside. You need to build into the organization the processes and structures that will support the culture change and outlast some of the inevitable turnover that any company experiences, particularly in retail.

"The mystery visits, which we will do on an ongoing basis, research, and the subsequent use of a gender lens over the whole face-to-face customer experience were milestones for the company. Our new business model has no choice but to become more women-friendly," Dostie asserts. "Now we're starting a group of women directors to talk about how we can work together to build an internal network, but to also figure out ways we can help the organization to better understand women customers." This kind of forum can help to keep the work alive, fresh, and current, and keep the women in these senior roles engaged in the work.

Donoghue adds, "At this point in the game, it's tough to quantify operationalizing gender intelligence, but it's made us think very differently. To me, that's a really big deal. The work we have undertaken has been massive. All those things that we think of in terms of the gender lens are way high up on a priority list."

Today, Allstate tops second or third in Canada in terms of their return to investors over three years. And it's not that there are that many new drivers every year. As Donoghue puts it, "Every time that you grow your business, someone loses. This is almost a net sum-zero game. I win, you lose. But our results are absolutely top shelf and adopting an internal gender lens was a really big part of that."

And to think that a major part of this came from thinking like a girl . . .

CHAPTER SIX

Controlling Your Company's PESTs:
Product Development Through a Gender Lens

Sometimes I can't figure designers out. It's as if they flunked human anatomy.

—Erma Bombeck, American Humourist

Okay, here's where you get to roll up your sleeves and get to play in the dirt. Let's assume the groundwork has been laid in getting your company change-ready. Your gender lens is polished and ready to roll. Where first?

Ask any organic farmer, and they'll say you need to start with the bugs. Farmers will be the first to tell you that unless there is proper pest control, the best leadership, knowledge, or strategy won't amount to a hill of beans. Think of a gender lens as internal pest control—a company mechanism designed to identify and control the retail vermin that drive women to distraction. As we previously mentioned, in our world, PEST is an acronym for:

- *Product/service development*
- *Environment (store/office)*
- *Sales and communication tools* (Internet, advertising, database marketing)
- *Training* (sales force)

TODAY'S WORLD OF ONE-DIMENSIONAL PRODUCT DEVELOPMENT

Some of the more cynical in our crowd would argue that gender-intelligent product development is an oxymoron. The world abounds with examples of products that didn't even glance in women's direction. We're still waiting on that women-sized automotive crash-test dummy, even though women actively buy half of the cars sold and influence 80 percent of the overall number of cars moved in car lots. In Canada, we enjoy Employment Insurance, but anyone owning more than 40 percent of the shares in his or her own company can't qualify. (They have the power to lay themselves off.) Unfortunately, EI is the vehicle through which maternity benefits are provided, leaving Canadian women business owners with bupkes if they have a baby. Clearly this is not something that affects men who own businesses. Lifejackets for women made an appearance only very recently (within the last five years), even though you'd be hard pressed to find a more glaring example of, uh, "gender difference." It's not like women have only just discovered this strange substance called "water."

So just how can people shake themselves out of this collective one-dimensional product-development malaise? Can it really be that hard to actually analyse the perspectives of what *both* women and men need/want in a product or service? How do you integrate gender intelligence into product development? Here's everyone's favourite answer: It depends.

IT'S THAT LEADERSHIP THING AGAIN

To begin with, gender-intelligent product development is a comprehensive process that needs to be "owned" by someone who will lead the way with their actions if they have any hope of the process succeeding. At some point, leadership needs to direct the functional group to add a gender lens throughout the product design and buying process. The group needs to start with making sure that everyone who touches product development (especially company leadership) actually considers *all* aspects of what the company offers, not only how both women and men interact with it, but the context in which they interact with it. Of course, not all women want the same thing, but there are some pretty basic premises to consider, such as body size, time issues, relational view of the world, and so on.

As for body size, promise me you won't get Sean started on this topic. He is continually bombarded with complaints from women around what is considered "normal body size." He is convinced that women's issue of finding decent-fitting clothes wouldn't exist if it were men doing the complaining. "I work with designers who know they have a legitimate problem on their hand. They often throw up their hands in despair. 'Impossible!' 'Too many variables.' 'You can't please everyone.' Designers shrug and point out that this person exists 'off the normal size curve,' you know, that one that is young, tall, and slim, almost downright pubescent. There seems to be a real reluctance to tackle women's fit issue. Underwear is a classic example. Men's underwear cost a third of what women's cost, but is more complicated to make. The peephole requires more patterning and sewing, but we take the accommodation of the male appendage as a matter of course. So why don't we seem to have this design challenge around building men's peephole? It's evident that the industry is perfectly capable of accommodating different sizes and requirements. Companies do this all of the time when they need to or they deem it necessary."

This leads to the next point around how to quell that product-development pest: You also need to be conscious of possible personal values and judgments that may filter out ideas for products or services that women consumers want. Getting this right requires equal parts of will, imagination, and brain cells.

WHO'S DRIVING THE PRODUCT DEVELOPMENT TRACTOR?

The question remains: Do retailers or manufacturers drive product development? In most cases, it's the manufacturer, but that doesn't mean you can't have an independent product development strategy or vision. Fulfilling the strategy means going up the supplier chain and getting manufacturers to give you what women consumers are asking for. As the retailer, you need to be in control of this.

Going back to The Home Depot, "Good Lord, in the beginning, hammers were delivered in pink," Annette Verschuren laughs. "My women merchants [buyers] were insulted. They went to their bosses and told the guys, 'Make it smaller and easier for me to grip. That's how to get women.' The guys got it and went back to the manufacturers. We don't get pink hammers anymore." Verschuren has always stayed close to the vendors and talked continuously about The Home Depot's gender-lens strategy for gaining market share. She explains: "You know it's the old 'You get what you ask for' routine. You have got to ask the manufacturers to develop product that is relevant to the customer that you would like to attract. And they'd better listen because, at the end of the day, we are the ambassador to the customer."

The Home Depot takes it even a step further and actually negotiates how the products are to be displayed. Verschuren says that "Women want to see the big picture, not a collection of disparate pieces. They live life relationally. The display formats we used were all wrong. Take Alexandria Mouldings, for example. We got them to change their entire product presentation to accommodate how women make decisions. Now women can actually see how mouldings are related to other elements and how they fit into the full context of home life. We talked to all of our manufacturers and got them to provide displays women customers can touch. If we didn't drive this, the displays never would have been created."

Regardless of where product development lives in your company or the process you use, there are three crucial areas to remember if you want to create relevant products that resonate with women and solve their problems.

1. Women will not change their perception that they aren't being taken seriously until the design of the product and services actually reflects their needs/wants/biology. Relook, redesign, and realign your product with a gender-based filter.
2. The market research stage will sink a product faster than a steel hammer if the research isn't conducted to reflect and accommodate women's world view. You also need to be sure you are doing the *right* kind of research.
3. You need to keep it real. Make sure a gender lens is anchored solidly throughout each of the development stages. What you are creating needs to solve problems. Keeping it real means you understand that gender-intelligent product development doesn't stop once the widget or service is created and is finally in the warehouse or office. Both the sellers and purchasers of the product need to be communicated with in a gender-intelligent manner.

USING A WIDE-ANGLE GENDER LENS IN PRODUCT DEVELOPMENT

- Can you articulate women's experience with your product?

- Could women's perspectives/experience of the product or service be different from men's?

- Is there any *disadvantage* to the product or service for one or the other gender? If there is, how do you handle it?

- Do you have gender-intelligent people, skills, and resources to make the product or service succeed?

- Are women involved in the design process?

- Do your sales and marketing departments include users of the product?

- Does it deliver more value to women customers than do competing products?

- Do the key drivers of the organization—executives, buyers, and store managers—demonstrate and understand gender and diversity issues?

- If your buyers are men, do they use a gender lens to ensure that they reflect women's needs in their buying decisions for the organization?

- When your organization communicates with women, does it understand how women's environmental, health, and time concerns and challenges intersect with the product or service offering?

IS YOUR "PRODUCT IDEA BANK" GENDER INTELLIGENT?

It really doesn't matter if your product is Blue Jays baseball caps, houses, or snowshoes, development must include a conscious, strategic discussion around how your product or service addresses *both* genders' requirements. But it also might be time to pull not only your product and service, but also your "product idea bank," through the gender-based filter. Most sources for new concept ideas originate either from internal sources—designers, engineers, manufacturers, and salespeople—or external sources—customers, competitors, distributors, and suppliers. That's a pretty deep pool, one that may be filled with people not all that diverse.

While women's reality remains disproportionately misrepresented or invisible in product development, men's changing reality must also be acknowledged and properly represented. Men's roles and societal expectations of them have altered enormously over the past couple of decades. Said another way, the world has changed. Have you and your product and service offering changed along with it?

> Regularly check the assumptions that you have traditionally held about your offering.

Here's an organization that anchored its growth strategy in dusting off a very male-skewed product, hauling it through a gender lens and re-creating it so it would appeal to women.

TAKING FLIGHT: THE BLUE JAYS

Coming in from left field (literally) is Laurel Lindsay. As the vice president of marketing for the Toronto Blue Jays, Lindsay is one of a handful of women executives in Major League Baseball. On meeting her, you'd realize that Lindsay has no problem holding her own in the male-dominated sports world. Her razor-sharp wit is a great equalizer. She parked all traditional assumptions about her very established, very traditional, very male product and threw open the window of possibilities. Her gender lens and the hard work of her organizational team literally saved the organization's proverbial bacon.

It's textbook: A product-oriented marketing strategy targeting an already converted audience. The 2004 marketing tagline was "You gotta see them play" and was designed to reach existing sports fans, mostly 40-year-old men. It was a successful approach back in the days when the team was winning and people viewed attending games as the "thing to do." Then the Blue Jays tanked. "You gotta see them play" sounded like a punchline. The product wasn't there anymore and the Jays were losing not only games but market share. It was a wake-up call.

Enter Lindsay. In 2004, when she returned to the Blue Jays from maternity leave, she was greeted by an attendance crisis and a low marketing budget compared to other teams in the league. (Baseball is not a huge pastime in Canada so there are additional challenges in marketing baseball in this country that you don't have in the US.) Since the Jays were underperforming, marketing to a performance-driven audience of sports fans was a waste of money. The net of it was this: Lindsay knew the growth needed to come from somewhere else.

She explains: "When you put all of your eggs in one basket and focus on the performance and tell people, 'Come see us because we are going to win' and we don't, you don't deliver on the promise. You alienate a person from coming to a game who couldn't care what the score is, but is coming for the experience. I believed we needed to rekindle people's passion for the experience. We needed to refresh our focus and recognize markets and the industry changes. We were not growing ticket numbers by continuing to preach to the converted."

Research had been done that indicated spending habits regarding leisure dollars, who made spending decisions, and what those decision makers were going to do. As well, research had been done on the aging fan base, and the fan base was not growing in terms of age and gender. Lindsay understood that a strategy that focused on the decision makers could help bring the turnaround in attendance that the Jays were looking for. Focusing on the future was her other strategy. She wanted to develop the fans of tomorrow.

Knowing that in sports the best experience is always with a capacity crowd, she proposed a strategy that not only would focus on women decision makers but also on the kids, which would bring out entire families. Her proposed strategy of targeting moms versus the traditional baseball fan was met with some silence in the boardroom until she explained the rationale. There was a lot of concern about alienating the traditional sports fan if the focus was on gender versus overall consumer potential. Fortunately, reasoning overcame reservation and management gave her the go-ahead.

Lindsay realized that if the club marketed the experience and emotion of attending a sporting event, they could grow the fan base beyond just sports fans, who in general come to see winning teams. But it is the role of marketing to sell the experience regardless of the score. Lindsay has always had a strong conviction that sports, especially baseball, is much more than just what happens on the field. It's a social and family activity. She also knew that it was women who made decisions about family leisure activities. Her goal was to have a visit to the ballpark placed alongside other leisure choices. In fact, she wasn't competing with other sports like basketball at all, but with the amusement park or the beach—she was competing for the consumer's time and wallet. She helped the club flip an attitudinal switch and her role then became not marketing a sport, but an experience.

Lindsay focused the media buy and promotions around women. The media strategy was to capitalize on the co-viewing habits in areas like youth TV programming, where mom and child watch together, and on Life and Entertainment sections of the newspaper, where people turn when planning their leisure time. She expanded beyond the traditional sports-centric media buy, one that focused on the sports pages or sports radio/TV channels. Her radio buys were female-centric and focused on selling a Jays game as a destination.

They introduced programs supported by a targeted media strategy such as "Ladies Night Out" (a program designed to bring women to the game) and "Babies at the Ballpark" (focused on new moms and their babies, featuring things like turning down the volume in that section and providing a shaded area of the stadium complete with bottle warmers and change tables). The attendance and revenue for each of the programs have quadrupled since their inception. Then came "Jr. Jays Saturdays" and the creation of the "Kids' Zone."

One of the things that Lindsay focused on was bringing more balance to the product offering, which was heavily skewed toward the male consumer. If women are in the ballpark, they will be doing most of the buying. Since they are more likely to embrace the entire experience, fans spend more on merchandise, etc., when their kids are at games, something their research supported. Jr. Jays Saturdays has a much higher proportion of sales than a Friday guys' night out. Not many guys will pick up a Jays pennant and then go out to the bar afterwards. While the family fans come less often, proportionally they spend much more per visit on higher-margin products.

Lindsay by no means ignored the traditional side of the business. She just plugged into the demographic rhythm of who was in the marketplace. She'll never run a moms' night on a Friday because this is usually guys' night out. Same drill with Saturday as Jr. Jays Saturdays, something we'll speak about first-hand.

For research purposes, Sean and I decided to take our families to check out Jr. Jays Saturdays. Have I mentioned Sean has four kids between two and eight? Six kids in total (my daughter and a friend), along with four adults, headed off on what was to be a wonderful family adventure.

As we manoeuvred through the massive crowds of excited kids and parents to get to our seats, my mind was racing with the mantra "This is going to be fun, this is going to be fun, and this is going to be fun . . ." Getting through the crowds was shockingly easy. It's what happened after we sat down that aged me 20 years. Let me preface by saying Sean is literally unflappable, a highly prized trait in a father of four. I, on the other hand, live in a constant state of flap. Plus, I am not good in a crowd of 10, let alone 37,000 (30,000 of which are probably under age 12).

We sat down and the kids were assaulted with every conceivable confection ever invented. And oh, my nerves, they actually bring it to you! (All you need to do is be sure you've disposed of the majority of your assets in order to pay for it, but that's another book.) Here's the problem. We have always been very diligent about the food Kate eats. She didn't touch sugar until she was four. We loosened up considerably as she got older, but this is a kid who still eats organically, including her Gummi Bears. The first words out of Kate's mouth after we sat was an astonishing "I wanna hotdogpopcornlicoricechocolatebarpretzelFreezee!" My husband and I just blinked. And smartly, said yes.

There was a good balance of kid-inspired stuff happening, but not enough to detract from the fact you were actually there to watch baseball. (However, my daughter complained, "Mom! You said there was kids' stuff to do here!" I sighed as I reminded her it was a *baseball game*.) They had kids announcing the player lineup from the announcer's booth, and more kids interviewing players, all of which you could see on the Jumbotron. The best part for me was watching the camera pans of the audience. The kids' reactions when they saw themselves on the enormous screen were hysterical. (There's a ham in every one of us.) The font used on the screen is adjusted to be a more kid-friendly cartoon-type, and a few cartoons are thrown in as well. Of course, no game is complete without the excitement of the wave and the seventh-inning stretch.

However, many kids (like mine) aren't like Lindsay, who at six years old dutifully filled out her scorecard alongside her father." Baseball is a long game and kids need other distractions. Lindsay has produced a Jays passport that has stamps kids can collect around the ballpark. It's a scavenger hunt–like activity that fills your book with stamps with the goal to collect a prize (given regardless of completion). It creates a challenge and distraction for the restless kid.

There was also the Kids' Zone so that you are surrounded by like-minded people and do not feel like you are an imposition to other fans. Also, everything in there is free. The Zone comes equipped with PlayStation machines; a jungle gym–type of maze; a virtual-reality pitching cage, which shows how fast and accurate you can throw; and, a virtual-reality hitting machine. There are usually as many men lining up to show off their prowess as there are kids.

The only complaint I have is that there was too much marketing to kids for my taste. Between innings they had some poor schmucks dressed up as gigantic chili peppers. The three of them attempted to run a race, but two of them never made it to the finish line. Much to the kids' delight, two of the chili peppers were too intent on pummelling each other. Very cute and pretty funny. However, the race was announced from the Jumbotron as the "Ranchero Chili Peppers" and the whole thing turned out to be a commercial for a salsa company.

After the game, they offered the kids an opportunity to run the bases, something every single one of the 30,000 children took advantage of. We waited 45 minutes to do a 34-second activity. Okay, I realize I'm sounding very Grinch-like here. Lineups destroy my will to live, but this appeared to be worth it. To be honest, it was "way cool" to be standing on the field with the fake grass and dirt.

I watched the faces of the parents as they left the game, eyes glazed from fatigue, a permanently etched grimace approximating a smile, shoulders stooped, hair frazzled, head buzzing, and wallet undoubtedly lighter. The kids? Same (minus the wallet), but from sheer delight, sugar, and eye-popping, synapse-exploding stimulation.

As Laurel Lindsay points out; it's about the *total* experience, and she couldn't be more right. Later that night, I overheard Kate telling a friend on the phone about her experience at the game. "I had two hotdogs, a Freezee, a bag of popcorn, and I ran around the bases!" Zip about Frank "The Hurt" Thomas's ankle injury or the Jays' 8–2 slaughter of the Orioles, but she still can't wait to get to another game.

A COLLABORATIVE APPROACH TO PRODUCT DEVELOPMENT—GENDER-INTELLIGENT MARKET RESEARCH

It's important to figure out how to talk with women on women's terms. You need to stay close and provide a two-way communication system, one that respects the way she sees the world, which may be a departure from how things traditionally got done. It is important to make it easy for her to give you feedback in the store or office and when doing market research.

All too often, companies either don't go to the source—women consumers—to find out what women's relationship is with their product or service, or they conduct their research without a gender lens. As good as a company's intentions might be, market research conducted without this perspective can fail entirely, at worst, or fail to yield the deep consumer insights one can achieve when using a method that captures gender-based influences.

We think of market research like a conversation. Your approach needs to reflect that women experience the world differently from men. Most market research is conducted and interpreted without a conscious gender perspective. Consequently, you may run the risk of having an unconscious male bias (a very common business perspective) seeping in.

Remember from Chapter 2 that women and men differ in how they process information, with men *eliminating* and women *integrating*. To recap, women, on average, don't think in a linear, step-by-step fashion as men do. Women's thinking resembles webs of interrelated concepts, not straight lines. Don't think for a minute this doesn't impact how she interacts with you, your product, and your market research process.

A GENDER LENS ON MARKET RESEARCH

- Are you evaluating the product or service to identify impacts to women and men (e.g., collecting data and statistics that take both women and men into account)?

- Is your research data broken down by gender?

- From the outside: Are you talking to women consumers?

- From the inside: Do you have a gender-intelligent team to interpret the research?

- Have you observed women's experiences with your product or service in settings similar to yours?

- Can you assimilate information from various sources in your organization?

- Can you showcase examples of action taken based on feedback from women consumers?

Women rarely take turns talking, they share more/deeper when a relationship has been established, and because they consider many more variables than men do, their actual "brain processing" time can be longer. When speaking with women, using the standard "sit down, scarf down a stale sandwich, go around the boring, square-boxed, one-way mirrored room, take turns answering generic questions, one hour later, boom! you're out the door" research approach is a waste of precious resources.

The Listening Event

We use a research technique called the listening event, something we've nicknamed "The Anti-Focus Group Focus Group." Listening events are structured to draw out feedback and feelings that are unlike anything you've ever heard in a traditional focus group. The key to achieving authentic and profound consumer insight with women is to understand how the role of "relationship" plays out. The quickest way to facilitate the necessary intimate atmosphere—the kind that allows the deepest insights to be revealed—is to have a small group of women share a high-quality meal together. Women have a thing about good food, especially when shared with good company, whether strangers or friends. The other thing that's needed is time, and lots of it. Our listening events clock in an average of three hours per session. In these intimate gatherings, generally involving no more than eight women, we are able to zero in on specific challenges and insights. We have found that a relaxed, comfortable room (which immediately knocks focus group facilities out of the game) goes a long way to generating the most authentic discussions among women. What a randomly chosen, 43-year-old Canadian woman sharing a leisurely, three-hour meal with other women in intimate surroundings can bring to light about a product or issue is quite astounding.

Asking the Right Questions the Right Way

While the "environment" is central to the success equation, it's also critical that you start with appropriate assumptions about the problem/question. If gender-based influences aren't considered properly, the research may miss the mark. If researchers know little about how to interpret gender-based marketing research, they may end up with the wrong information, accept wrong conclusions, or spend more money than they need to.

The issues here can be as simple as the survey questions used. While close-ended survey questions have their place, it's important to know their limitations when it comes to gender. They offer only fixed possible answers so people can't respond in their own words. These leading questions and limited responses can completely miss gender-related issues if the issues aren't built into the offered answers. On the other hand, open-ended questions can create an opportunity to converse about an issue from all perspectives and angles, especially in a listening event scenario.

Interpreting the Answers the Right Way

Especially where gender is concerned, we have seen evidence that people may start with a bias that colours whether they accept or reject the research results. In fact, human nature dictates that people often tend to accept results that show what they expected and to reject those that don't meet their expectations. Here's another way to put this: Market research data, in and of itself, does not "say" anything; only people do. Researchers and facilitators need to be highly skilled in looking for innuendo and pay attention to gender-based sensitivities, historic or otherwise.

THE BEST MARKET RESEARCH: STAYING CLOSE TO YOUR OWN CUSTOMER

Staying close to women customers provides the best kind of market research. The important thing is that something gets done with the information, both subtle and direct, that women are providing you. Your culture should encourage employees to develop a "radar," one that can help gather and provide this feedback. Women consumers provide a wealth of information at the front line in terms of the types of comments they make and the questions they ask.

> "Do you have this in x, y, z?"
> "I saw this item at another store and I am looking for something similar."
> "I need to solve this problem. Do you have something that will do that?"
> "I'm buying this for a member of my family."

These questions provide information about what women are looking for, what they are interested in, and who they are buying for. The challenge becomes how to collect and relate this information back to the organization. The first step is to value this information and the person who brings it forward, whether a customer or employee.

It's easy for managers to get frustrated, as often this information is presented in a way that is not readily useful. The front-line manager needs to ensure that he or she is not a bottleneck to getting this information forwarded to head office departments. Head office also needs to get involved—usually achieved by visiting the stores or offices and interacting with women customers.

FRONT-LINE EMPLOYEES GET FEEDBACK AND INFORMATION FROM CUSTOMERS ALL THE TIME.

• How does the company receive this information?

• What do they do with it?

Can I Tell You About Colour?

Gender-intelligent product development is not just about getting it right but what happens when you get it wrong. Sean likes to work in all areas of the store, especially during peak traffic hours on weekends. He says, "I learn more about how the business is running and what is happening with our customers in a couple of hours than I could by doing days of focus groups.

"For example, colour is a big issue at MEC in terms of cost and risk factor. More colour options = more fabric = more cost = more risk if the colour doesn't work out.

"One day I got into a conversation with an enthusiastic customer who was asking about the colours of our winter apparel lineup. I was hearing the same refrain about our colour selection, not new, but still important to listen to. I listened to her constructive criticism about our women's colour options and combinations. We were actually pulling clothes off the racks, comparing different companies' products, identifying colours that worked, didn't work, and why certain colour combinations were better than others. I told her that these colours were ordered far in advance of their actual production, and that sometimes it was hard to predict what colour was going to be in demand. Her response said it all. She had purchased a Lululemon jacket years ago that she still received compliments on to this day. It hit me like a bolt of lightning. Great colours stay great, rarely getting tired or old. This reinforced my desire to get this colour thing right. There has to be a way to combine 'function and fabulous.'

"Although I didn't make the sale that day, I built up more goodwill that, in the long run, would serve us well. In relationships, women don't expect things to be perfect. They do expect to be listened to and, more importantly, expect the store to respond. Another woman came in having made her own modification to a kid's snow pants to improve the cuff of the pants. I immediately credited her with a new pair of snow pants (her son had outgrown the old pair) and I sent off the pants to our kids' apparel product manager. We made the change to all of our pants the following year."

CLOSE THE FEEDBACK LOOP

- Make it clear when employees join your company that one of their functions is to share product/service improvement ideas up the chain. Reward employees for doing this well.

- Use conference calls to exchange ideas and information between store and head office staff. Make them presentation-based to allow staff to view again afterwards.

- Working on the sales floor is essential, so executives need to get the heck out of the office and spend time working on the floor. This signals to the staff the importance of the customer to the organization.

- Create a number of ways that customers can provide input into your product and service offering. Conduct passive and active surveys; for example, conduct exit interviews as consumers leave the store. Provide locations in the store or through your website for feedback/ comments. Divide the comments into product and service suggestions and have the *entire* management team read them. They then can act on any that pertain directly to their area of focus.

- Make sure management reports back to the staff on the status of store-level recommendations. They need to see that feedback is taken seriously.

Understanding and staying close to the customer is the mantra of Calgary-based Shane Homes. This company not only created a product through the eyes of women, but is remarkably diligent about the gender lens they use in market research.

STAYING CLOSE TO THE CUSTOMER: SHANE HOMES

In 2003, I got a call from Shane Wenzel, senior VP of sales and marketing for Shane Homes. He was interested in having me speak to his group on how to better meet the needs of women customers. He wryly observed, "I have never sold a house just because it had a great workshop or garage." He knew women were the major influencers of home purchases. And while his request was not unusual, the results of the day we spent together certainly were.

We pulled together staff from different departments of the company, including senior executives, sales, marketing, design, and operations. A pivotal moment in the session occurred when company owner Cal Wenzel and his son and company namesake, Shane, experienced their epiphany. One of the exercises I had people undertake was to design a home as best they could through women's world view. It then dawned on both Wenzels that while the decision makers in home purchases were usually women, his designers (along with the entire industry) were men. There was no gender intelligence influencing the designers' work.

This is one of the things I love about working with smaller companies. There were no committees struck to conduct feasibility studies on the merits of creating a committee to investigate the possibility of researching further the need to better understand women consumers. I swear, by the end of the day, everything was decided. The Shane Homes project was not only going to have the floor plan designed by women from start to finish, they were actually going to build the darn thing.

Shane Wenzel explains the company's journey to becoming a gender-intelligent retailer. "The research that Joanne provided us in the workshop revealed that single women buy more homes than single men, and that women in families do most of the house hunting. We also knew that women tend to spend more time in the home when there are children, so they have stronger opinions on what features they would like in their home. All of this, combined with the fact that women control 80 percent of the consumer dollar, produced a great incentive for us to design a home for women. We decided to ask women specifically what they wanted."

Add to this the power of observation. Shane Homes watched how people actually used their product. They looked at the context it was used in and with whom. They scrutinized how the product fit into women's lives, and what job it did for them. They wanted to see if people were using the home features as they intended or if they were making adjustments to make the features work better for them. Observation in context provides necessary insights in new product development.

The company conducted listening groups over an eight-month period with a group of 10 women who had recently built new homes. Since these women had just built homes, they had a clear picture of what they and their families wanted. They were asked what additional features, including floor plan, layout of rooms, window and door locations, etc., would benefit their lifestyle. Shane Homes documented their wish lists and had one of their draftspeople incorporate their ideas and design several floor plans. Then they took the floor plans back to the group for feedback, returned to the drawing board, and repeated this process until they came up with something that everyone was happy with.

Much to my mother's delight, the new model homes were named Yaccato 1 and Yaccato 2, with the latter and the larger of the two unveiled in December 2004. "This idea and the name of the model were inspired by Joanne Thomas Yaccato," says Shane Wenzel. "Some of the unique features incorporated into the Yaccato 2 include even small items that are virtually unnoticeable when walking through the home, but that make life simpler and thus more enjoyable."

For example, the spacious mudroom offers a storage organizer where family members can hang their jackets, shelves to put their shoes on, and cubbyholes for mittens and scarves, with convenient access to a laundry room with sink. There is a large walk-through pantry that houses wood shelving and an upright freezer, with lots of room to store the small appliances and offering convenience when bringing in the groceries after shopping. The women expressed the desire for extra storage space and more work areas in the kitchen since they spend so much time in this room and like to keep it organized. Shane Homes put in deep pot drawers, a space-saver microwave, and extra counters and cupboards. There's even a vegetable sink on the island with a garborator. A home management centre in the kitchen with built-in filing cabinet for further organization also provides a space where children can work on the computer while under the watchful eye of their parents. Other neat features include a sink tilt-out tray for storage of soap and scrub pads, a motion sensor light in the pantry, and awning windows that can be left open for fresh air even when it's raining. The second floor includes two bedrooms of equal size for kids (eliminating some squabbling in room selections), a family room with vaulted ceiling, and a convenient IT centre.

. Shane Homes went on to win both a single-family award and the award for Innovation in the 2005 Alberta Awards of Excellence in Housing by the Alberta Home Builders Association. Yaccato 1 and 2 homes have been built since 2005 based on their original design; however, Shane Homes also now incorporates a number of these options into their standard plans or at least offer these items as options to customers.

For all of you wondering about a home designed for men, Shane Homes is a step ahead of you. They also built another model using data from a male perspective. Wenzel says, "This was easier to do as most homes have always been built with more male than female influences, so the changes were less dramatic. And yes, the garage was huge and there was a TV in almost every room . . .

"We are always ahead of the pack because we stay very close to the customer," Wenzel explains. "We go through the gender-lens exercise on a regular basis in order to stay up to date with what customers want. We have expanded the areas of research to include women's needs during the sales, construction, and service processes. The original 10 women now act as an advisory group, along with new participants who are consistently added to the mix, which keeps us plugged in and current."

KEEPING IT REAL THROUGHOUT THE ENTIRE DEVELOPMENT PROCESS

The last point on product development we need to make centres on keeping it real. Successful companies know there is an advantage to learning what women and men want and need from the product/service rather than trying to persuade them to buy what the company happens to be producing. When you are designing and launching a product that is focused on meeting women's needs, it's essential to think about it in terms of how the product will not only offer an experience but provide an authentic solution. It's imperative to move away from a purely unisex, attribute-based product development and selling (good-better-best, etc.) approach. Keeping it real means you've also figured out how to talk in a gender-intelligent way, both to the people selling and the people buying the product.

Mountain Safety Research is a company that not only put their product through a rigorous gender-lens exercise, they maintained a "solution" lens throughout their entire process. They went the distance in terms of ensuring everything that touched the product—technical specs through to language on packaging and sales training—was gender intelligent.

GENDER INTELLIGENCE FROM BEGINNING TO END: MOUNTAIN SAFETY RESEARCH

Mountain Safety Research (MSR) is a company that takes product development very seriously. They build equipment for people who are outdoors in some of the most extreme conditions and *need* their products to perform. They also manufacture some of the most popular snowshoes in North America. The company invests heavily in product research and development before they bring a product to market. It's not just about selling product, but selling a product that keeps the users *safe* when they participate in outdoor sports.

The snowshoe business was new for MSR. However, with its mandate of innovative and meticulous product design and development, this was an ideal opportunity to try out some new thinking in a market dominated by technology that was hundreds of years old. MSR also realized the demographics were changing, as boomers were looking for winter activities that didn't have the same hip-breaking hazards as skiing. Boomers wanted to stay active and take advantage of low-impact aerobic activities.

MSR started with a unisex snowshoe. While the new design was popular, the company quickly realized a serious shortcoming. They had assumed the market for snowshoes would be men. Turns out it wasn't. With other outdoor sports, the male/female split was two-thirds male, one-third female. The chart below shows a different reality for snowshoeing.

	% Male	% Female
Backpacking	67	33
Climbing	67	33
Snowshoeing	60	40

Source: MSR

Snowshoeing had lower entry barriers as a sport, and there was a full spectrum of age ranges of women participating. This was a market begging for attention. The product development people had bells going off in their heads, so MSR went back to the drawing board. Because they were focused on women's needs versus just the product, MSR made some interesting discoveries that ultimately led to their success.

Lee Getzewich, product specialist of MSR Snowshoes, says, "MSR learned some time ago that—surprise, surprise—men and women *are* different. The advent of women-specific products in the outdoor market started taking hold over a decade ago, and as this momentum continued to build, we realized we needed to address the needs of these consumers more directly, rather than continuing to apply a one-size-fits-all approach."

There were a couple of sources for what women needed and wanted from MSR in terms of its products, some formal and some informal. Getzewich says, "We spent a lot of time talking to consumers, at retail stores, and events, and trade shows. But most of our detailed knowledge came from extensive field research working with a PhD biomechanical gait specialist. From this research, we were able to understand the more subtle differences between men and women, stride length, foot position, gait mechanics, and apply this knowledge to the specific design features."

With this market feedback, they began their investigation. Getzewich explains: "Our initial product was unisex. We then introduced the Lightning product line after analyzing the biomechanical gait of the sexes. We learned that there are attributes that are unique to men and women." The Lightning product line was a complete redesign. There were several competitors that offered snowshoes for women, but the Lightning product line offered a totally new experience for women because of these gait considerations.

Extra care was given to the design of the women's shoe to make it ergonomically correct for specific challenges that women face when snowshoeing. Women, because of shorter average heights than men and a walking gait that put their feet closer together than men, found that snowshoes were too big overall and too wide to walk on snow with ease.

The women's models of snowshoes were narrower overall, patterned differently to allow for greater ease of walking (narrower through the tail of the snowshoe versus men's), and the harness used to connect to the snowshoe was designed for women's smaller and narrower feet.

A BIOLOGICAL/SOCIOLOGICAL LENS

- Does the development of the product/service incorporate appropriate biological/sociological differences between men and women in the design?

- Is colour your main point of product differential? If so, why?

- Does the product reflect women's different life stages and is it relevant through those stages? If not relevant, why?

- Women go through more significant physiological changes during their lifespan than men. Is the product relevant/supportive of this?

- Is the product designed with a benefit in mind that will answer some of the key questions for women—health, making life simpler, fulfillment?

- Does it address some of the life realities/opportunities for women? (They own more small businesses; are more active, older, etc.)

- Can it support her many roles, including that of primary caregiver for aging parents and family?

- Does it pose a win/win outcome or an ethical solution, or does it "do good"?

- Does it help women share and satisfy their demand for information?

- Does it address women's personal and family safety concerns?

- If you're a financial institution, does your approach reflect women's view of money as a medium of exchange or a tool to purchase, rather than power and status?

Communication with their internal (dealers) and external (women consumers) audiences was the next step for MSR. Education became a big part of their communication strategy. MSR spent as much time thinking about how they would communicate the changes to their dealers and customers as they did in developing the product. There was a lot of effort in getting out to the stores and educating the front-line salespeople. In North America, MSR made the snowshoes available to sales staff at their retail partners at special prices so staff could try out the equipment. So, when customers inquired about snowshoes, the staff were able to talk informatively about the product.

Some of their retail partners offered how-to-snowshoe clinics for customers to support the launch. Carol Blaydon, spokesperson for MSR, says, "We are a product-driven company first, and marketing comes second. Marketing has to support product development. MSR developed in-store collateral brochures that included lifestyle imagery of women. The tone, the language, imagery, etc., all played a role in the launch. We vet many of our product ideas and marketing messages through consumers before the final launch. The company is full of women, as well, who are never short on opinions."

The imagery on all of their collateral materials was carried through on their website. No specific advertising was done to launch the women's line. MSR relied mostly on the in-store experience and word of mouth.

The women's shoes were priced the same as the men's shoes, and both were priced to compete with competitors' high-end models. For women used to having to pay more for "made-for-women" equipment, this was a bonus.

Another gender-specific approach MSR used was to empower women with information. To help the decision-making process, gender differences in product design, rather than the usual technical specifications, were articulated in plain language on the packaging. (When a product is designed and developed based on sound principles of legitimate differences, then a lot of the communication effort can be left up to the product.) The company also spent a lot of time designing and labelling the packaging. They choose a neutral red colour for the women's product.

The Lightning Ascent product line of snowshoes has contributed tremendously to the company's growth in this category. MSR had very aggressive sales targets. Their goal was to increase the value of sales globally by 50 percent. They achieved this and are securely in the number-two spot.

As you can see, developing a gender-intelligent retail ecosystem doesn't mean making the experience more feminine but rather focuses on what is driving the purchasing decision for women and integrating it into your entire business process. This is a crucial element in the product development realm. When developing a product, *be* the product and ask yourself:

- Why would women choose me?
- Why would women keep me in their life?
- Why would women recommend me to someone important in their life?

CHAPTER SEVEN

Controlling Your Company's PESTs:

The Store Environment

In department stores, so much kitchen equipment is bought indiscriminately by people who just come in for men's underwear.

—Julia Child, Chef, Author, and Television Personality

WOMEN AND YOUR PHYSICAL SPACE

Women consumers have this "radar" that some call intuition. We call it biology. Women have wider peripheral vision and can process many things at once, including non-verbal cues. Details about things like lighting, smell, colour, tone, texture, warmth, music, and salespeople come rushing in in one great swoop. When a woman walks into a store or an office, first impressions come at her like a shout rather than a whisper. In a nanosecond, she's able to answer the question "Is this a place where I would (voluntarily) spend time?"

While the store/office environment is the physical space in which you operate, like your salespeople, it's also the billboard that advertises your company's gender intelligence. The physical retail environment includes both tangible and intangible components that interact to create that whole first impression. If there was ever a place to dump that file-folder approach to business, this is it.

In retail, your physical space is a crucial component of the larger "ecosystem" of a woman consumer's experience: your brand, your website, the conditions within your trading area (area of competition), and her needs and aspirations. It is the one place where you as a retailer have the greatest control. Ecology is a helpful way to think of this interaction. The principle of retail ecology is that you demonstrate an understanding about the entire experience, both the little things (like the cleanliness of washrooms) to the big stuff (such as meeting or exceeding women's service expectations).

We mentioned earlier that to create a gender-intelligent retail ecosystem, you need to break down the individual components of the physical space, use a gender-based filter, and then put the pieces back together again.

Our research revealed that women, much more so than men, wanted to see an accurate reflection of their lives in a retailer's approach to advertising, products, services, and *store design*. A good understanding of consumer needs is a strong driver of loyalty among both women and men, but women are more likely than men to seek out retailers who consider all their needs, including family needs. "Making life simpler" resonated much more strongly with women than men in our research. The floor of the store/office is a perfect place to drive home that "make life simpler" mantra.

Retailers need to expand their line of vision around the customer experience in the very tangible sense of physical space. An excellent example of this was revealed during time-motion video studies of shopping behaviour done by Paco Underhill's company, Envirosell. It was discovered that all retail space requires a deceleration zone. This means that people will walk about 30–40 feet before they slow down enough to start absorbing the information around them. There is a pedestrian walking speed and a shopping speed. Most retailers know this, but they can't resist sticking stuff right in the front of the store. This might make sense from a planning point of view. However, watch people walk into a store; they will miss everything within that first 30 feet.

Companies need to dump that whole short-term "sales per square foot" mentality. There's tremendous benefit in creating a balance between "productive" and "non-productive" areas. Our research further reveals women not only notice but want amenities like family washrooms, kids' play areas, and community and learning areas. This creates powerful passive public relations benefits and contributes to a more productive overall retail environment.

Your customers need to feel like you designed the place for them; they can find what they need, they will have a good experience, and then they come back. You need to ensure that navigating your store is intuitive, staffing is optimized to provide quick and efficient service, and product placement makes sense and is easily understood. Equally important is to make sure you have good recovery systems when things do not go well.

While none of this is new, reframing the process with a gender lens offers possibilities previously unimagined. In the product development chapter, we shared a series of questions that need to be asked in order to be sure both genders' requirements were being included. It's the same for the store environment, which needs to take into account both the obvious and *hidden* infrastructure, and view it all through a gender lens: change rooms, merchandising strategy, washrooms, store/office displays, reception area, parking, lighting, seating, wayfinding, ergonomics (height of shelves or desks, width of aisles, weight of doors), and customer service.

Before you close this book muttering, "Who's got the budget for this?," recognize that this doesn't have to be a huge physical retrofit. There are countless examples of stores and offices that have achieved a decent gender-intelligent environment with a reasonable budget by simply tweaking, redecorating physical space (including washrooms), creating play areas for kids, opening curtains to bring in natural light, and so on.

No matter which way you come at this, you need to know how women and men are different at the floor-of-the-store level.

THE MALE BEAVER AND THE FEMALE OCTOPUS GO SHOPPING

Women and men move through retail spaces in relatively pre-set ways. In our beaver and octopus analogy in Chapter 2, we discussed how men focus on and isolate the one task that they are given. Women will move through much more of your retail environment and process the experience quite differently.

We met Dr. Raymond Burke, professor at the Retail Management School at the University of Kansas earlier. He describes the process like this: "In shopping, there is the objective experience relating to the physical store (is it hot or cold?) and the subjective perceptions in terms of their enjoyment of the experience (good time/bad time). Then there is the subsequent impact on behaviour in terms of the purchase. My goal is to try and link all these things together so I can figure out how to better convert demand into purchase."

Dr. Burke believes that people's perception of a retail experience is actually directly connected to the tasks they are faced with. For example, the purpose of the trip (women's trips tend to be more for fulfilling immediate demands than men's trips); the experience level of the shopper (women are more experienced shoppers than men); and the criteria that they use for shopping (women generally use more criteria than men). Dr. Burke completed a survey in 2007 that tracked 5,000 customers in more than 15,000 shopping trips focusing on superstores and supermarkets. Customers completed an extensive exit interview about navigation, service, time/effort, level of clutter, etc. This is what he found (a few things we've already mentioned earlier in the book, but are also relevant here):

- Women find the shopping experience less enjoyable than men do if there is a lack of available seating, refreshments, and clean washrooms.
- Women are more sensitive to what varies across stores (things like pricing, design, selection).
- Women interact much more with the product throughout the store and also cover more of the store's territory.
- Men tend to touch items on the lead fixtures (front of store), sweep through the store to the back of the clearance fixtures.
- Women process a lot more information when they shop. They are able to put together more clothing combinations from different parts of the store that were not necessarily connected through the display. They are more organized, more purposeful.
- Men are generally able to make a purchase decision in less than 60 seconds.
- Women's average purchase decision lasts four minutes.

Dr. Burke ascribes some of this to the fact that women act more like professional shoppers in terms of how they approach the task. Women are more methodical, reasoned, and aware of how to navigate a retail environment than men are.

Another interesting observation that Dr. Burke provided was the impact of women in group shopping or social shopping. The more social a shopping experience, the higher the conversion rate (buying something), and the mere presence of women within a shopping group had a significant impact.

- Individual men have the lowest conversion rate, at around 15 percent.
- Groups of males have a slightly higher rate, around 22 percent.
- Male/female, individual female, and female/female have a conversion rate around 30 percent.

In other words, as soon as you add a woman to the group, her role as key decision maker and influencer kicks in and the conversion rate goes up.

So what are the key elements to pull through the lens when looking at your physical space? In this chapter, we've focused on what we know to be key issues for women:

- Wayfinding
- Lighting
- Ergonomics

- Washrooms
- High touch combined with high technology

Wayfinding

It seems to Sean and I that most companies build stores and offices from the inside out. The problem is that women shop from the outside in. We are always in places we are not familiar with when conducting gender-based store/office analyses, so we are very sensitized to directions and wayfinding signage. We spend a lot of our time dazed and confused because many companies haphazardly add on signage in a mish-mash way.

Some say wayfinding is not only signage but also the overall architecture; lighting; placement of store paths, racks and shelves; and merchandising. The women in our study were really clear that *all* of these things combined to not only help them to find their way, but decide if they would stay. Women don't just read "the sign," they look for information from a range of visual cues: how you organize your product, how the aisles are laid out, how you highlight or accent with lighting, as well as the information offered. Sean adds, "For men, you just need a big sign."

So how do you create gender-intelligent wayfinding? Start by asking yourself the following questions:

- Can your store/office be easily found?
- How easy is it to find your way around? Is the store layout, selection, and product placement intuitive to women?
- How are women being guided through the store?
- Where is the washroom located? (Better not be 40 miles north of nowhere.)

- Are displays used to help navigate through the product assortment?
- Is the signage placed in clear sight lines?
- Does the signage broadcast women- and family-friendly amenities?
- Does the signage use symbols/pictures to help convey information?
- Is accent lighting utilized to draw attention to relevant information?

Signage

From a woman's perspective, most signage that we've seen is too text heavy. Women are very visual and integrate information really quickly, something companies would do well to remember. There's a reason for the "Golden Arches" or Allstate's "You're in Good Hands." It's an easy-to-see symbol that everyone recognizes. Sean suggests, "Use clear and bold signage outside and twice as much as you think you need. I learned this the hard way. We had a visiting VIP from head office who missed the Toronto Mountain Equipment Co-op storefront, almost a full block in length. She walked right by it." Think of the exterior of the store like the runway beacon for a plane. You want to gently guide the plane to its destination, not turn on the lights at the last minute. Entrances need to be distinguished by both architecture and signage. The building and parking lot need to easily reveal where the entrance is.

When you use a gender lens on basic wayfinding principles, you start to think of signage that describes the types of amenities available: family washrooms, parking for families, covered/underground/valet parking, drive-thrus, store hours.

Ensure your signs are visible in all conditions, including day and night and different times of the year.

And Yes, Women Do Ask for Directions

Here's something else: Women will actually call in advance and ask for directions. Landmarks are really important when giving directions. A piece of public property is probably worth more as a wayfinding device than the most expensive sign that you can buy. Use those public visual cues when providing directions on your website or on the phone.

Safe Parking

The function of good design is to meet consumer needs in the simplest of terms, which includes the outside surroundings of your space. There's a retail developer from Winnipeg whose attention to the detail is so evolved that it included the slope of the parking lot. He wanted it adequate enough to drain off water, but not so steep that shopping carts or strollers take off, careening into parked cars.

Well-lit parking is mandatory for safety reasons. There should be no parking spots or areas where women might be vulnerable when they are hidden from view. Some stores offer an escort to the parking area, something that is hugely appreciated (or downright weird to some women consumers). The parking spaces need to be large enough to accommodate minivans and car doors that are opened wide to remove children from car seats. There needs to be enough room between rows so you can easily back up from your parking space and not risk an accident (or a major neck sprain). Of course, there should also be dedicated parking areas in front of the store for parents with young kids and those with restricted mobility.

It's also important to note that parking isn't just about cars. Have ample drop-off spots for shopping carts in the lot so customers don't have to walk back to the front door while the kids sit alone in the car.

WAYFINDING CHECKLIST

- Your exterior says a lot about your interior, don't overlook it.

- Provide clear wayfinding information from the street and from the car to the front door. Good wayfinding makes life simpler.

- Be conscious of the perceived and real safety of your location. Make women feel safe: discreet security patrols and panic stations, parking near entrance and exits, and bright lighting so there are no dark corners.

- Transition areas from parking lots or the exterior need to be accessible. Get rid of those insurmountable sidewalk curbs—think of strollers and wheelchairs.

- Have preferred parking for parents with small children.

- Ensure that entrances are clearly demarcated, day and night.

- When giving directions, use public landmarks and visual cues; they can be as important as expensive signage.

- Make sure store employees are adept at providing *correct* directions.

Lighting, The Natural vs Artificial Debate

Women will react more positively and spend more time in the retail environment if there is more light. However, *natural* lighting is something we humans appear to not only be intuitively drawn to, but thrive in. A study, *An Investigation into the Relationship between Daylighting and Human Performance*, revealed that skylights were positively and significantly correlated with higher sales. All other things being equal, an average non-skylit store would likely have 40 percent higher sales with the addition of skylights, with a probable range somewhere between 31 and 49 percent.

Beyond the energy savings, Wal-Mart discovered this benefit of natural lighting. In their Lawrence, Kansas, store, they found sales in the naturally lit portion of the store were twice that of the artificially lit section. They also found that the cash registers under the naturally lit portion rang in twice as many sales as the artificially lit ones.[1]

Retail expert Paco Underhill says, "When I go into Neiman Marcus, I usually find a big skylight somewhere and it floods the store with natural light. Natural light sends a message; it says, 'We spent some money.' It's ironic that sunlight is more expensive looking than electric lighting, but it's true."[2]

The business case alone is compelling for natural light, but if you combine this with what we know about women consumers, introduce as much natural light as your building situation will allow. Denis Gervais, president of GHA Shoppingscapes, says, "The quality of lighting and colour rendition for women is more important than it is for men. Women's sensitivity to colour is much more developed. They will ask to take a garment to see it under natural lighting. Women are more discriminatory in their purchases and will analyze the garment prior to making a purchase. The colour rendition and light levels are critical in the

1   http://www.buildinggreentv.com/keywords/natural-light
2   Paco Underhill, *Call of the Mall* (New York: Simon & Schuster, 2004), 174–175.

decision-making process. The male purchase is less of a process and more perfunctory."

At the end of the day, though, you can only do what you can only do. If natural lighting is not an option, a well-lit environment is still crucial. Women shoppers like to see where they are going and can take in more at once. It also makes the store appear cleaner. Women also look for prominent signage and like to inspect merchandise to a greater degree than men do, something good lighting supports. It also helps them keep a better eye on their kids. Whether natural or artificial, a well-lit store is generally more conducive to a happier customer.

LIGHTING CHECKLIST

- Include natural lighting wherever possible.

- Fix the lighting in areas where women look in mirrors. No one is a fan of that ghoulish shadow effect.

- Think of lights like paint—they can complement or compete with what you are trying to do.

- Go for balance and aim—either highlight or wash an area.

- If the scale of the project is big, use lighting designers.

- Consider lighting that will show what colours will look like in natural light, especially in dressing rooms.

- Bright is right, especially in the northern regions of North America in the winter.

- Women may not notice, but Mother Nature will. Your electricity bill will be lower if you choose environmentally friendly options like T5 fluorescent lights, LED display lighting, low-wattage halogens, and photosensors that dim lights whenever it's naturally bright.

Ergonomics

The Ergonomics Society of Europe defines ergonomics as the fit between people, the things they do, the objects they use, and the environments they work, travel, and play in. If good fit is achieved, the stresses on people are reduced. They are more comfortable, they do things more quickly and easily, and they make fewer mistakes.

Whenever humans interact with physical things, there will be ergonomic considerations—for example, the size of a gas pump handle, the height of a shelf, the size and weight of a package, the weight and force required to open a door, the height of a desk and chair, or the polish/finish on a floor. But from a retailing standpoint, gender-based ergonomic considerations is often a truckload of "uh-ohs."

The crux of it is this: Most spaces in the public sphere are designed around the physical specs of men. The height of shelves, the average weight of exterior doors, the height of door handles, and even the size of chairs are based on embedded design principles that were developed from a male perspective. Natalie Bely, an architect friend of ours, confirmed our suspicion when we asked her what the "standard" was for dimensions of things like doors, counters, and the height of cabinets. "Buildings architects tend to use a fairly rough estimate of a 6-foot-tall human, with eyes at about 5'6". This gets used for window location, kitchen counter heights."

If women find they are reaching, pulling hard to open doors, or finding it difficult to grip things, the chances are good that it's because of design failure—that of the default "standard" being 6 feet tall. This is not a treatise to take on the design world, but rather to apply a gender lens to specific areas where you have some control, things like the height of a shelf.

Decent Washrooms

When it comes to washrooms, Sean is pretty knowledgeable. There is no full-time custodial staff at MEC, so he gets first-hand experience if something goes wrong during the day. He says, "Doing washrooms well is not easy and takes a lot of work to maintain, but they are an essential part of the experience and must be handled competently."

Washrooms are pivotal to women's initial impressions of your business and can be a strategic asset or a PR nightmare. Sean is absolutely convinced that women will spend more time in your place of business if the washroom is decent. They need to be accessible, easily found when you first walk in, clean, and provide basic amenities, especially change tables. Our research reveals that women (and growing numbers of men) are beginning to have an expectation of a family washroom, one that allows for strollers to be brought in, as well as hands-free features in faucets, soap dispensers, and toilets.

You may have physical limitations in your physical space, but there are ways to get creative. We know of a do-it-yourself clay pottery store where the owners were stuck with a basement washroom. They brought their creative touch to decorating the washroom, using bright colours and their own artwork. Washrooms present a captive audience with opportunities to talk about who you are and what you do. Choose what's appropriate and look at it as an opportunity, even if it is just to display your brand in some way.

WASHROOM CHECKLIST

- Have a proper baby-change facility in *both* washrooms, and *don't* stick it inside the handicap bathroom stall. It shouldn't be treated as an afterthought.

- Hands-free features for faucets, paper dispensers, and air dryers are preferred. Use high-pressure air dryers—they are the only ones that really do dry your hands. Dyson (the vacuum people) make the best Sean has seen on the market.

- Match the washroom decor to the store (unless the store is done in an early garage-sale motif) and use as many durable materials as budget will allow. This area often takes a pounding because of frequent cleaning and cheap materials.

- Carefully consider the design and construction. Have more tiles and less drywall, accent lighting, and fixtures that are easy to clean like wall-mounted toilets.

- Use ambient and accent lighting to create a softer lighting versus overhead fluorescent lighting.

- Cleaning should be done on the hour in a high-volume environment, but the minimum is once a day.

- Have a separate family washroom that accommodates a stroller. Add a child-restraint seat for toddlers. Without this, when moms need to use the washroom, they can have an awkward situation on their hands when the toddler learns how to open the main washroom door.

- Of course, washrooms must be wheelchair accessible.

Combining High Touch and High Technology

There are some distinctive differences between the sexes in their *expectations* of technology, but Dr. Burke found differences in *preferences* for the use of technology as well. He found that while technology plays a role, it is a combination of high-touch and high-tech measures that improve the shopping experience for people, especially women. Women have a greater appreciation for any technology that increases the convenience of the shopping experience, but they still want to interact with sales associates, much more so than men. They also want the ability to connect with a customer-service representative, even when online.

Here's where women's time issues really come into play. All of the research reveals that women consumers will use technology in the purchasing process, but one of the main criteria is that it *must* make their lives simpler. Men, it seemed, expressed a greater interest in using various types of technology for technology's sake, regardless of if it adds convenience or saves time.

Burke explains: "Men and women had distinctly different views of what would constitute an ideal shopping experience. Men were more positive about using the Internet, cell phones, mobile and palm computers, and interactive kiosks than women. In contrast, women shoppers expressed a greater interest in being able to use catalogues at each stage in the shopping process: to learn about new items, search for product information, compare brands, and make purchases. In a nutshell? Women want technology that leads to convenience and speed, anything that is going to help with navigation, faster checkouts, ordering items out of stock, etc."[3]

But it still needs a human touch.

Sales Promotion Technology

Dr. Burke's study also showed that in both online and in-store shopping environments, women are consistently more focused than men on price, promotions, and coupons. When online, a greater percentage of women said that they must have product prices, a list of sale items, personalized discounts, and the ability to view prices and print out coupons for the local retail store.

When asked about their ideal pricing policy, women were more enthusiastic about variable pricing strategies, including high-low pricing, end-of-season markdowns, and even daily and hourly promotions displayed on electronic signs. They were also more interested in receiving email notification of sales. When shopping in conventional stores, women wanted printed circulars and store signs listing promotions.

The lesson here is that you need to treat women as professional shoppers. They are more likely to move to a different store based on price, but at the same time they are also looking for efficiency. Make women's lives simpler and save them money and you will have a winning formula. Do only one or the other and you may win some of the time, but not all of the time. What Dr. Burke's research shows is that women are open to new and inventive ways to deliver pricing strategies.

---

3   Dr. Raymond Burke, "Technology and the Customer Interface: What Consumers Want in the Physical and Virtual Store," *Journal of the Academy of Marketing Science* Volume 30, No. 4 (2002): 411–432.

Point-of-Sale Technology

Women specifically preferred having a real cashier to scan, bag, accept all forms of payment and provide a printed receipt, rather than a fully automated system.

Point-of-sale (POS) technology used to be in the realm of low tech, but is now high tech. Today, you can purchase something at Northern Reflections or Addition Elle, have your customer numbers entered, and your loyalty account pops up. You don't have to carry 9,000 cards with you. Another key consideration is a retailer's ability to integrate POS data, website data, and overall customer data and have the integrated summary available at the retail point of service. This is a good indication of their sophistication, something we'll touch on in the next chapter. There are ways POS data can be utilized to help companies understand women better, an opportunity used not nearly enough.

Self-Help Kiosks

Are they appealing to women? It appears to be situational. Women will be just as quick as men to use the kiosk to buy a movie ticket or order food if there is an enormous lineup. However, most women prefer real people to assist them in all parts of the sales process. For women, the best consumer experience incorporates both high tech and high touch.

Burke's research showed that women have a greater interest in using kiosks offering electronic coupons that are automatically deducted at the register. Interestingly, convenience store ("c-store") retailers in the United States have been using this type of technology to help drive repeat purchase and loyalty. A few years ago, Tennessee–based Calloway Oil installed coupon dispensers at its gas pumps. The investment to do so was hefty—about $4,000 at each of its sites—but in one month the chain printed at the pump and then redeemed in-store 1,672 coupons for free milk and 1,800 coupons for a free pint of ice cream. This increased foot traffic into the store and created better sales in higher-margin items, which quickly paid for the initial investment. Burke says, "The kiosk technology should be integrated into the store displays and merchandising to strengthen rather than compete with the store's brand identity."

Burke offers this advice: "Every retailer is in a unique situation with unique assets. One must resist the temptation to use off-the-shelf technology to create a generic customer impression and shopping experience. The technology should reinforce a retailer's brand heritage and leverage its distinctive strength. Generally, though, the application of technology has to be well thought out and include women's perspective. Unless it adds value to the overall shopping experience, it won't be a good investment."

HIGH TOUCH/HIGH TECH TIPS

- Don't offer technology for technology's sake.

- Ensure your technology makes it easier for customers *and* easier for your business. It needs to do both.

- Present customers with the option of dealing with a live person.

- Offer technology that provides the ability to compare products, brands, and pricing.

- Position your technology to act as a productivity tool for the professional-woman shopper.

WOMEN-CENTRIC STORE LAYOUT STRATEGIES

1. Scan your environment for high-contact areas for women and scale furnishings accordingly. Focus on areas such as mirrors, the seat height in change rooms, and washroom counters.

2. Look at doors, especially exterior doors, and automate them to make them easier to operate.

3. In an office environment, look at desk and chair heights, especially during a sales transaction, and adjust accordingly.

4. Maintain the balance between productive and non-productive spaces at a 70/30 product-to-amenities ratio in terms of square footage.

5. Tilt the ergonomic considerations of the floor set-up toward women. Men will not complain about a rack being too short, but a woman will complain if it's too tall.

6. Ensure the product layout and design is logical from a woman's point of view, not from a product manufacturer or a two-dimensional plano-gram perspective.

7. Build and design green wherever possible. Following the principles of green design will lead to a more natural and productive environment just by virtue of the process. (More about this in Chapter 10.)

8. Ensure product adjacencies (what goes beside what) make sense from women consumers' point of view versus what makes sense from a store planner's point of view. For example, a woman making a peanut butter sandwich will want to see the peanut butter next to the jelly, not in the next aisle over.

9. Have merchandising that "explains" how different products work together, whether it is displaying clothing together or combining a

drill, drill bits, and tool belt. Good merchandising provides solutions to what women need.

10. Create merchandising that uses a variety of techniques to create visual interest within a store rather than row after row of shelving at · the same height.

YOU CAN START SMALL

If you do only three things that focus on gender intelligence in your physical space, make it the following:

1. Make the women's experience as seamless and convenient as possible.
2. Create visible clues that let women know they are welcome. This can be as comprehensive as a full store renovation or simple things such as a small sign and space that lets women know you welcome breast/baby feeding. These speak to all women whether they are at that life stage or not.
3. Eliminate obvious turnoffs such as stereotypical/demeaning depictions of women.

Of course, we wouldn't want you to hold yourself back. If you want to give men and women the ultimate retail environment, here's a table summarizing what will make them both very happy.

The Ultimate View of Your Physical Space as Seen by a Beaver and an Octopus

	Men "Eliminate"	Women "Integrate"
Location	The store is easy to access.	The store is easy and safe to access by car or public transit. Location allows for easy "trip chaining" (women connect errands together more frequently than men).
Wayfinding/ signage	Outdoor signs are big and bold. In-store sections are clearly identified.	There's an overall sense of welcome as the woman walks in. Outdoor signs are bright and inviting. Signage is legible and utilizes clear symbols versus text where appropriate.
		She can get the full mapping of the store just by scanning the signage at the top of the sections. She can navigate the retail environment easily through the clear presentation of product, signage, and displays. There is a logical flow to the product that assists in navigating through the store (e.g., the batteries for the drill they just bought aren't on the other side of the store).
Parking/ exterior	There's adequate parking. Sections are clearly identified so he can easily find his car on his way out.	There's adequate parking, with mom/baby–designated spots. Section identification is clearly marked. Parking spots are broad enough to accommodate minivans and wide-open doors while removing kids from car seats. Parking rows are spaced so it's safe and easy to back up.

(Continued)

		The parking lot is well lit, with no blind spots. There are many places where a customer can safely drop off her shopping cart without having to walk back to the front door.
Product assortment	Bestsellers are always in stock. Products are organized on hierarchical technical specs. (good–better–best)	There is a broader, deeper product selection that addresses women's complex lives and time poverty (for example, milk, tampons, diapers, pantyhose, *and* a decent cup of coffee). Product associations are not based on how a buyer/merchandiser purchases a product, but rather on how a woman might associate with the product. Product placement is intuitive and relates to women's mental map of looking for solutions. Product assortment is not presented in a hierarchical way, but how it's related to the solutions she seeks.
Displays	The store is orderly. Bestsellers are clearly identified and featured upfront. Products are touchable and can be *easily* put back.	The store must be uncluttered. Complementary products are displayed together or close by. Displays are family-friendly (what's featured at children's eye level won't shock or outrage mom). Create ideas and solutions by combining and demonstrating different products together. Inspire possibilities and allow interaction (i.e., displays are not static but can be interacted with and touched).

(Continued)

	Doors are easy to open	Doors are easy to open.
Ergonomics		Aisles are wide enough to naxigate strollers and wheelchairs.
		Top shelves are easy to access for a woman of average height.
		Heavy items are stocked on lower shelves. Floors have some cushioning to ease the pain of shopping in heels.
Lighting and ambience	The store is well lit. There are lots of mirrors.	There is natural lighting so women can get a better appreciation of the merchandise as it appears outside the store, especially with respect to colour.
		Music is appropriate and reflects prevailing general tastes.
		Lots of mirrors available.
		Lighting in the store is chosen appropriately, especially around mirrors, so that it will not cast unflattering shadows.
Change rooms	Enough change rooms are available. Men spend less time in change rooms, so the decor is not critical.	Change rooms are spacious and clean.
		The lighting in change rooms is flattering.
		Mirrors are located inside the change rooms and allow for a full front and back view.
Washrooms and amenities	Washrooms are clean and have baby-change facilities.	Easy to spot when you first walk in.
		Spotless, single-sex, and wheelchair accessible.
		There are proper baby-change facilities.
		Offer more than one stall.
		There's room to bring a stroller in the stall. No-touch features on the faucets, high-pressure hand

(Continued)

		dryer, and toilets are a serious bonus (provided they work).
Technology	Technology for technology's sake is okay. Men are comfortable being early adopters of technology.	Technology is used to facilitate and simplify her life. She can still connect with a customer-service representative if she wants to (combination of high tech and low tech).
Customer service	Service is quick and reliable.	Service is quick, reliable. Employees are genuine, welcoming and service-oriented. The sales process is focused on providing information so women can make informed decisions, and on relating and establishing rapport.

CASE STUDY: PETRO-CANADA GETS NEIGHBOURLY WITH WOMEN

Recognizing the Opportunity

We're going to take a bird's-eye view of a work in progress— Petro-Canada's new convenience store incarnation, Neighbours. Neighbours is the company's attempt to create an entirely new customer experience by developing a more upmarket, "Europe meets the gas station" kind of concept. They are using a gender lens throughout the evolutionary process of the store. Feel free to borrow what is relevant to your own situation. (Unless, of course, you're Shell . . .)

But first, let's pull the lens back and look at the industry as a whole, one that is firmly entrenched in conventional retailing practices. We did an industry analysis in the mid-2000s that evaluated which industries were perceived as making an effort to meet the needs of women consumers. Oil and gas finished dead last.

Industry Satisfaction Among Women*

1. Supermarkets and grocery stores	76%
2. Food companies	63%
3. Pharmaceutical and drug companies	61%
4. Restaurant and food-service companies	60%
5. Book publishers	57%
6. Cosmetics companies	56%
7. Hotels	54%
8. Newspapers and magazines	53%
9. Movies and videos	52%
10. Home electronics	51%
11. Banks	50%
12. Clothing manufacturers	48%
13. Telephone companies	46%
14. Hospitals	45%
15. Alcoholic beverage companies	40%
16. Car manufacturers	37%
17. Computer companies	36%
18. Exercise/fitness clubs	36%
19. Insurance companies	36%
20. Airline companies	33%
21. Car dealers	27%
22. *Oil and gas companies*	*23%*

N = 1,020
*Based on a five-point "agreement" scale.
Source: The Thomas Yaccato Group/Maritz

What's so odd about the oil and gas industry bringing up the rear is that they actually champion "making life simpler" with their convenience stores. The Canadian Automobile Association reports that women make significantly more trips than men to perform household-sustaining activities, such as shopping and family errands. As women have entered the labour force in greater numbers, more shopping and errand car trips are made during non-work periods, including peak congestion periods. Women (especially those with kids) are more likely than men to stop at multiple destinations and make more trips on the way to or from work.

Not surprisingly industry research also shows the genders aren't that different when it comes to their shopping lists—candy, snacks, and cigarettes. However, one of the best insights we had from our research came from a participant in one of our listening wants. The question was "What are the top three things you buy at a c-store?" The respondent replied, "What c-stores sell is not necessarily what women want to buy. They are the things that, in the past, we've been restricted to buy in a convenience store. If you offer me other things, my top three things to buy will change. My list today is a response to the parameters of what they presently offer."

A study by Clickin Research revealed the biggest differences between the sexes came in the form of safety, store layout, food quality, and motorist services. Also, women are more loyal than men. Although women tend to shop more frequently and at more and different locations than men, women are loyal to their c-store, so one could be forgiven for asking, "Why haven't these guys clued in?"

Well, they are most assuredly starting to. There's major competition going on in the c-store world right now, with everyone wanting to know how to bring in women. The industry is beginning to understand that women are a lucrative market, a serious departure from their 18–34 single male focus.

The C-Store Through a Gender Lens

When we do a c-store store analysis, we first deconstruct the typical gas/convenience store experience, in order to illustrate the typical kinds of things women come into contact with. Part of our process is to create a video or photographic essay of a store experience from a woman's point of view. This is designed to highlight, using a "hyper" gender lens, what is and is not working, isolating issues that don't always get picked up in a store-design process. We take a "logical path" approach and start with signage visibility from the street. We'll proceed to the pumps and fill up, then go into the store itself. We analyze everything from how easy it is to open the front door (keeping in mind that children may be in tow), to product displays. (Sean and I usually walk into c-stores with our hands over our children's eyes because of the T & A magazines and the dizzying array of candy, generally illegal substances in our homes.) Essentially, we look at everything from colour and lighting to the washrooms and everything in between.

An additional tool that we've developed is an amalgam of all of the women in our market research—Lori. Using a colourful but accurate narrative, I created a portrait of a typical day in the life of an average woman and how a gas station c-store could really support her. I'm always struck by the number of oil and gas executives who, upon reading the narrative, smile and say, "My wife tells me this about our stores pretty much daily."

Let me introduce you to Lori.

A Day in the Life . . .

Lori groans as she opens her eyes. Though the sunlight through the trees is heartwarming, the thought of tackling her enormous to-do list all but makes this Zen moment vanish. Her one-year-old is crying, the dog is barking to get out for her morning constitutional, her rambunctious five-year-old is jumping on her bed, and she has a major presentation to deliver to a client this morning. Her brain snaps awake and, with the precision of an army general, begins to calculate what needs to be done in the next hour: Make breakfast and lunches, take out something for dinner, sign that field trip permission slip for Sarah, remember to pick something up for the birthday party after school, feed and dress the baby and get his diaper bag ready before dropping him off at daycare, feed the dog, remember to organize the play date for after school tomorrow, put the finishing touches on the PowerPoint presentation for today, and make that doctor's appointment.

Lori takes a deep breath and leaps out of bed. She hits the floor running. An hour later, she's sitting in the driveway, exhausted; the kids are loaded into a filthy car; and she is running 15 minutes late. She makes a mental checklist of what needs to be accomplished in the next 30 minutes. Of course, she needs to get Sarah to school and the baby to daycare. Because it rained for three days straight, the car is simply filthy and she's got to get it cleaned before picking up her client at 9:15. She has to get diapers. She's dressed in her corporate navy blues, but, while wrestling with the dog to get her in her crate, she manages to get a run in her pantyhose. She hasn't had her coffee yet because Sarah used the last of the milk for her cereal. In fact, Lori realizes that she forgot to eat breakfast. Sarah is haranguing her about the gift she wants to give Ali at her birthday party after school and she has no clue where she will find the time to get it. Then she looks down at the fuel gauge—empty.

It's only 7:45 a.m., and so begins another day in the life . . .

She pulls out of the driveway while trying to remember if there is a gas station along the way. Lo and behold, up ahead looms a sign. She pulls in and joins the enormous lineup of cars waiting to pump gas. She unsuccessfully avoids getting dirt and gas on her well-appointed attire, but Lori does notice a convenience store across the parking lot. Daring to be hopeful, she mentally knocks off all of the items on her list that she might be able to buy. She's desperate for pantyhose and she only has an hour to get to the client's office. There are diapers, milk . . . "Heavens," she thinks to herself, "Do I even dare to imagine I could find something that might pass as a birthday gift? A car wash??? Maybe there might even be something healthyish that I can shovel in for breakfast? Please God, let there be a decent cup of coffee."

Lori drops her purse as she manoeuvres to open the heavy door while holding a car seat and a five-year-old. Sarah retrieves the purse and unceremoniously dumps it on her brother, who begins to wail. At that precise moment, Sarah announces she needs to go pee. Lori's muttering ramps up a notch. They walk in and immediately go into overwhelm. The first thing Lori sees, prominently displayed not 5 feet from the front door, is a huge display of the much-heralded *Sports Illustrated* Swimsuit Edition, the one with 12 topless models on the cover. The aisles between her and the kids and the washroom are crammed with every conceivable cavity-inducing confection known to humankind. The seeds of foreboding have now germinated into full-blown panic. Sarah goes absolutely wild in the face of all of the beautifully displayed, brightly coloured chips, chocolate bars, and sodas, her apparent need to pee somewhat derailed. Lori repeats the Serenity Prayer four times by the time they reach the washroom, which is filthy and out of paper towels. There is no change table. Lori stands there in disbelief.

But now the real fun begins. Top priority—pantyhose. In short order Lori discovers there are none. They have condoms, but no pantyhose. Lori and the kids are now standing in front of the diapers. "Thank God." She breathes a sigh of relief. "Damn, wrong size." No other sizes are stocked. "They'll have to do," she thinks resignedly. At that moment, Sarah pulls a package of condoms off the rack, which is strategically located at her eye level, and asks if she can have it. Lori snatches it out of her hands and tells her no. "What is it, Mommy?" she demands imperiously. "I want one!!!" Lori quickly redirects her attention.

Lori is nervous to stay in the store much longer as it is a sugar landmine, but she really needs to find a birthday gift. She wanders through the store, making sure she quickly moves Sarah past the T & A magazines. "Let's see, phone card? Not likely. Car wax? Maybe next year." Lori also notices that some of the merchandise is pretty dusty, contributing to the sense that stuff here isn't all that fresh. She quickly abandons the idea.

At that moment, her stomach begins to growl. "Breakfast!" she thinks. She takes a quick look around, hoping to find something—anything—that resembles healthy, whole food. An apple even. She spots some kind of deep-fry machine, doughnuts, sweets, some unappetizing sandwiches wrapped in cellophane. There's a fridge with some dairy products, so she opts for a large package of cheddar cheese.

Lori finally gets to the cashier and, out of sheer frustration, asks the young, bored-looking clerk why the items she was looking for aren't stocked and why the selection is so limited. "There's tons of stuff if I'm an 18-year-old single guy, for heaven's sake." He looks at her blankly and shrugs his shoulders, radiating an "It ain't my job or my problem" attitude.

It's now been 15 minutes and other than wrong-sized diapers, a hunk of cheese, and, thankfully, coffee, Lori feels no further ahead. In fact, she ventures, she's even *worse* off—cranky mother, cranky kids, time wasted looking for things that should be stocked but aren't. "Time is the one thing I don't have," she mutters to herself. "What a wasted opportunity." She still needs to stop somewhere to get the car washed and find pantyhose and a birthday gift. She heads back to the car, buckles everyone in, and heads off to the daycare, now quite late.

As she thinks about her morning, she begins to realize that this whole "gas station thing" meets the needs of people like her 18-year-old nephew Colin. His most-consumed food group includes trans fats and refined sugar. He never complains about pumping his own gas and putting in his own wiper fluid because he is rarely time-pressed and has no kids to wrestle with. He'd be the prime market for condoms and T & A magazines, but wouldn't clue in that they are displayed at children's eye level. He has yet to experience the 30 minutes it takes to get the kids to stop vibrating after visiting a store that resembles Willy Wonka's chocolate factory. He can buy car wax, but women can't buy pantyhose. In fact, he can choose from an enormous selection of car-related products, but you can't find proper-sized diapers. He washes his own car (a teenage-guy thing), a time luxury that women can ill afford, but car washes aren't at every gas station. The fact that gas station attendants are diffident or often seem terribly bored likely wouldn't penetrate Colin's awareness.

"I need a wife," Lori thinks to herself, feeling resentful that the term "wife" is synonymous with servant. At daycare, she looks around at the women. They look exhausted, their teeth are gritted, and their shoulders bunched up around their ears. She breathes a resigned sigh as she gets back into the car to get on with her day.

The Neighbours Story

Who among us is surprised that women consumers (with or without children) are a constituency that's begging for quick, reliable, and relevant service? As this narrative attests, the lack of gender perspective in store design and amenities, as well as product selection, can be jaw-dropping. Like most companies, c-stores could benefit from dumping that proverbial file-folder approach to retail that we described in Chapter 1 and begin a fundamental shift to looking at how things interconnect.

We were hired by Petro-Canada to look at their c-store concept, particularly Neighbours, through a gender lens. We looked at every touch point and pulled the feedback together to get a holistic view of what was being done right and what still needed work.

Phil Chulton, Petro-Canada's vice president of marketing, says, "While Petro-Canada's existing network was doing well—solid single-line growth in line with the market—it wasn't differentiated in the marketplace. We wanted to introduce a concept that set us apart from the traditional c-store offer, allowing us to leapfrog our competitors. We looked at a broad range of retailers to see what seemed to be working and what wasn't. We broadened our usual scope and visited traditional c-stores, department stores, and restaurants. By doing that, we found open, spacious, and well-lit stores to be the most appealing to customers. This became the basis for our qualitative and quantitative research."

Chulton continues, "Women are certainly important to the Neighbours concept, but we wanted to be sure we built a concept that appealed to all on-the-go, time-starved Canadians. There were several areas we knew we had to get right to appeal to women when it came to food and other services. This is where our work in design and functionality helped get us past the typical c-store gas station offer. We knew that if we were able to get the lighting, washrooms, parking, and product offer right, the things that women demanded, our stores would appeal to a much broader base than before."

So we began the gender-lens process by looking at Petro-Canada's conventional format called SuperStop, which has the classic c-store layout with a cash desk in front of a wall of cigarettes. The freezer runs along the back wall, and the aisles of dry goods and food are in the middle. Washrooms are, well, gas station washrooms. T & A magazines are in your face. Food selection is very limited. We watched a woman walk in at 8 a.m., look around for something to eat, and, after a little deliberation, plunk down a doughnut. Her attitude clearly suggested this certainly wasn't her preferred choice, but there wasn't much else offered.

Petro-Canada was only too well aware of shortfalls in this store concept in terms of design, layout, and amenities and wanted to create an alternative for those more discerning customers—women. This is precisely where Neighbours came in. Visiting these two stores—SuperStop and Neighbours—was like visiting a dollar store and the Bay.

While the company conducted the usual focus groups, they knew they had to go beyond that to really understand what drives customers. They conducted "ride alongs" in which researchers spent days with select guests (with their permission), listening to what they said, watching what they did, and noting how they lived. By observing people where they lived, worked, and played, Petro-Canada got a better understanding of what to look for in their stores.

Chulton explains: "From there, we built a full-sized model store inside a warehouse and brought in guests to try it out. They gave us tremendous feedback that impacted the final design. Now that the stores are in the field, the company continues to bring guests through to get feedback and improve."

With a gender-based perspective, Sean and I did extensive store visits and created a documentary with me playing the leading role as a customer. The goal was to reveal what a woman's experience might be when visiting Neighbours. We then conducted field research with groups of women who visited a variety of conventional c-stores, including Petro-Canada's SuperStop. Finally, we brought them back together in listening events to talk about their experiences.

We began the listening events by asking women to share their perception of c-stores. They were instructed to associate a colour with their conventional c-store experiences. It was pretty much universal—grey and dirty white. Women told us they believed they weren't seen as valuable or even desired consumers. They were clearly dismayed at a company's assumption that women would actually pay for stale, outdated, greasy food, and were quick to point out that the items they needed the most usually cost the most, while the stuff they wanted the least was what usually went on sale. They felt the stores weren't clean and the washrooms were "an abomination" and a deterrent to entering the store.

If I Could Design the Perfect Store . . .

So, we asked women to design their version of a decent c-store. Because we have done store visits with a wide variety of retailers, we can tell you with complete authority that most of what follows is applicable to *all* retailers. After dividing the experience into what goes on outside, then inside, and finally the amenities, this is what the women's "must-have" list looked like:

The Outside

Reaching women consumers starts with the site itself:

- I want to see the sign clearly when I drive by.
- It has to be easy to get to if I spot it at the last minute. I don't want to risk my life having to cross four lanes of traffic or pulling a U-turn.
- Make it safe by providing good lighting outside the store.
- Have lots of easy-to-read signs that tell me what's offered so I won't waste time.
- Create a welcoming, well-landscaped outside environment.
- I want lots of glass to let in natural light.
- Make it warm and inviting.
- Have adequate parking with a mom/baby–designated spot.
- Provide a drive-thru option and a car wash to save me time.

- I may have children with me. Make it easy for me to get into and out of the store.

The Inside

- I have to get what I need quickly and easily.
- Offer merchandise that is relevant to my life *as well* as your T & A magazines (if you must)—decent selection of pantyhose, birthday cards, healthy emergency lunch stuff.
- Be a legitimate source of fill-in shopping. Offer fresh produce as well as healthy meals and sandwiches. Dear Lord, kill the microwaveable burrito.
- I love loyalty programs and free stuff.
- Display merchandise in a way that makes sense. Putting Ambesol and condoms together is confusing. And just plain weird.
- Give me new ideas by using grouped displays.
- Do not charge me the equivalent of the national debt for a package of cheese.
- When I stand in front of 30 varieties of chocolate, I'm weak. Mix it up more with fresh and *healthy* food options. (Beef jerky does not qualify.) Display the healthy food more prominently.
- I hate to ask someone to reach something for me. I hate bumping into stuff with my stroller. I hate having to drop everything to open a stupid door that's too heavy.
- Ambience is huge. I like natural light and soothing colours. Don't set my teeth on edge with elevator music or loud rock music.
- Give me a comfortable place to sit and eat if I choose to stop long enough.

Washrooms

- Spotless, with no-touch features on the faucets and toilets, is a serious bonus.
- Dump unisex washrooms. "It's just too gross for words."
- More than one stall. Please.
- It must be wheelchair accessible.
- Washrooms needs to be inside your location, not outside or 30 miles down a dark hallway.
- Make sure men get to have fun changing diapers.

Technology

- Make sure that whatever technological gizmo you have makes purchasing fast and easy, but I want a "real person" option as well.
- If you are absolutely convinced that you no longer want to provide a polite young man to fill up my tank, make the process easy and clean. Right now it's pretty disgusting.

Customer Service–Focused Staff

- Hire people who take pride in their work and don't radiate the "This is a dead-end job" attitude.
- Make sure they are knowledgeable enough to provide quick resolutions to my problems.
- Train them to be customer-service representatives, not order-takers.

This list provided us with what women were looking for, but we also had a list of our own. In advance of the store visit, we asked ourselves these questions:

- Women have preferences and need space and relevant amenities. How will Neighbours address this?
- Women lead complex and multidimensional lives. What has Neighbours done to help make women's lives simpler?
- Women are generally health-conscious, ethically minded, and holistic in their consumer approach. Will the store experience support this?
- Women integrate information from many different sources; they are looking for not only *what* is being sold but also *how* it's being sold. How has this been integrated in the presentation of products and information and the customer service?

With a fistful of pocket money and our group of women, we set off on another field trip to the local Neighbours.

What We Found at the Neighbours

Exterior Environment

The goal of the service centre concept is to move a customer from the gas transaction, which is a low-margin traffic builder, to the high-margin profit centre. The challenge becomes how to do this and make the store concept appealing enough that it will draw people inside the store.

Right off the bat, most women in the research spontaneously commented that the Neighbours sign was bright and inviting and created an impression of openness, a sense of "Come on in and have some really great food." There was a food menu at the pump listing a wide selection of salads, freshly made sandwiches (on the spot), panini, cappuccinos, and lattes. The exterior of the building was attractive and had uncluttered, large windows to give a sense of what was inside. There were automatic sliding doors and parking spaces in front. The women actually said they were "overwhelmed in a good way."

In some locations, they offered a drive-thru, providing options and solutions for people with children in the car. All of these improvements are important differentiators and create a very strong impression that there is a significant investment going into making the environment more pleasant. Even from the parking lot (which offered lots of spots), women said, "Well, well, well . . . Petro-Canada might actually get it."

Wayfinding

In our research on what women wanted from a c-store experience, they said that easy wayfinding would be a distinguishing feature. They wanted to see better organization of the store, perhaps with stations for food prepared by real people, an area for lottery tickets, one for automotive goods, etc. When the women visited the new Neighbours store, they were pleasantly surprised. Signage made counters easy to find. They noted that all they had to do was scan the top part of the store and in a flash had the full mapping of the place.

Not only were the women struck by a well-organized store, but by the large assortment of fresh and healthy food, including fruit, organic tortilla chips, even homemade soup. While there was still an abundance of sweet stuff, it didn't bonk us over the head.

Lighting

One of the very first things women did when walking in the store (after commenting on the wonderful smell of the coffee) was to exclaim with delight about the natural light and big windows. This was in contrast to many convenience stores where fluorescent lights blind you, turning you that ghastly green. They even went as far as to comment how the lighting worked beautifully together with the overall colour scheme and textures.

Ergonomics

The doors at Neighbours didn't require the strength of 10 women to open. In fact, they opened automatically, a bonus if you were carrying a baby in a car seat. The shelving was placed at a height such that it did not block the view of the entire store, which made all of the items accessible for a women of average height.

However, Neighbours is also a gas station. There are some external ergonomic considerations that apply to any self-serve gas station. It is a messy job, especially in winter with the amount of road grime collected on cars. The ergonomics of the pumps are designed for an average male build of 6'0" and 160 pounds, so the handles are too big. The height and distance between the pump and gas tank are awkward for women who are shorter. The window washers have short handles that require most women (who have shorter arms) to reach over the front hood of the car, getting filthy in the process. Refilling windshield-wiper fluid and oil is an awkward task, especially performed in heels and dresses. And those caps on the wiper fluid? What the heck is that!? I gave up counting the number of manicures ruined or spills on my clothes.

Although the full-service format is becoming extinct, there are still ways that an organization can demonstrate it understands women's "ergonomic" problems and frustrations. While there are instances where you simply can't make adjustments to the service offering, often there are low-cost solutions. For example:

- Gas stations can place paper funnels by the gas pumps.
- How about disposable gloves so I can wear something to protect my hands (and my expensive manicure) from the gas? Provide a reusable product like gardening gloves as an option for the more environmentally conscious.
- Offer tips and tricks for refilling wiper fluid, filling the gas tank, etc. How about a simple plastic stepping stool so I can reach over the hood when I'm washing the windows? Yes, they will get run over, lost, or stolen, but the last time we checked, they cost about $5.

This isn't rocket science but rather common sense. But it needs to be the kind of common sense that emanates from adopting a gender lens. If you are designing something new and from scratch, then it's obviously easier to incorporate a gender lens into the design process (remember Allstate). But there are lots of opportunities with your existing space if you just widen your perspective a bit.

Decent Washrooms

In our preliminary c-store research, women told us that clean washrooms would make or break their experience, making a big difference in whether or not they would spend time in the store. If the washroom didn't make them faint dead away, they might consider getting a sandwich and coffee and even browsing around to see if they needed anything else. If the ambience and amenities appealed to them, they were quite prepared to spend some time in the store. That's a big departure from rushing in, grabbing what they need, and getting the heck out.

Petro-Canada created a very different washroom experience at Neighbours. The washrooms were clean and had a decor that actually matched the rest of the store, which created a more harmonizing aesthetic. There were hand-free features in the washroom that made it easier to use and an all-round cleaner experience.

We were intrigued to note that most women commented on the accessibility for people in wheelchairs (one participant has a child with a disability) or others with mobility issues, including young children, even if it didn't reflect their own life situation. Women also wryly noted the separate male/female washrooms, saying the other configuration (the dreaded unisex) would have been completely unacceptable. A huge detractor (and disappointment), however, was something so fundamental: no baby change tables in either washroom.

Combining High Touch and High Tech

Neighbours offered an excellent blend of high touch and high tech. They introduced computer kiosks that allow customers to select their sandwiches and other food, right down to adding or subtracting toppings and condiments. Research shows that women respond overwhelmingly positively to pictures, colours, and charts, especially if there are lots of choices. The photographs of the food on the screen, especially the wide variety of options, were very appealing to women. Some of the women pointed out that this type of system can make ordering easier for a wider range of people, particularly those who do not speak English as a first language.

While there were a couple of people who grumbled at the technology, most had a lot of fun using it. (The concern generally was around taking too long and holding people up.) However, having the high-touch element—staff—there to help made the detractors much less grumpy.

The women told us that they prefer to deal with someone face to face versus simply paying at the pump. But the typical c-store experience did nothing to encourage them to go into the store, so they avoided it. There was consensus among the women that the staff in convenience stores seemed utterly stuck. Several women talked about how seeing these people made them feel sad. They felt the staff consisted of new Canadians who seemed stuck in dead-end jobs and were thus devalued.

The staffing strategy was clearly different in the Neighbours stores. The staff was very customer-service oriented. Staff smiled, welcomed people to the store, and helped out with the computer ordering system. It was also noted that there seemed to be more staff than in a typical convenience store. This was a good thing, as it made the women feel safe and there was a lot of positive energy in the store.

Just the Right Colour

If you remember at the beginning of the chapter, women associated the colours of grey and dirty white with the conventional c-store experience. The colours used to describe the Neighbours shopping experience were warm yellows, oranges, and earthy browns. Women's previous knowledge of Petro-Canada was uniformly an association with gas, while the name "Neighbours" conjured a much wider range of ideas that referenced a sense of community.

The best compliment Petro-Canada got occurred when the women in the study tried to define Neighbours. They couldn't. Responses ranged from "a farmer's market gone high tech" to "this is definitely not a convenience store."

Enough said.

CHAPTER EIGHT

Controlling Your Company's PESTs:

Selling and Communication Tools: Getting Women to Listen

If we sometimes don't get a reaction from our customer, it may be because we've put her to sleep.

—Title9Sports www.titlenine.com

SELLING TO WOMEN IS MUCH MORE THAN YELLING

As with all parts of the ecosystem, unless a company has a gender-intelligent leader with a vision around how to talk to women in a way that doesn't have her screaming for the mute button, the proverbial needle will never move. In fact, it really hasn't moved. It's the exception rather than the rule to see women intelligently portrayed in advertising or see consumer data that's been gathered about women used in a way that's actually relevant to her. Women typically describe companies as "circus barkers trying to get my attention."

With years of experience under our belt, we've been able to synthesize much of women's opinions on a wide range of issues relating to how companies attempt to communicate with or reach them. To keep it neat, we'll borrow the concept of the five Ws: who, what, when, where, and why.

1. Advertising is completely irrelevant to my life. Just *who* are these women that I keep seeing in advertising campaigns, posters, and sales brochures?

2. *What* exactly is the message that companies are trying to convey to me?

3. Just *when* might companies start using the truckloads of data that I've provided them over the years in a way that's useful to me? And I don't mean another bloody loyalty card.

4. *Where* do companies think I am? How are they trying to find/reach me?

5. *Why* am I still having this conversation?

This last question is a big one and we aren't stupid enough to try and answer it.

ADVERTISING: AN ENORMOUS PEST FOR MOST WOMEN

These days, advertising has become as much a science as it is an art. It's had to evolve because both the medium and the message have become as crowded as the Tokyo subway at 5 p.m. Rising above the fray is becoming a serious challenge, with companies and agencies resorting to more unusual means to reach people. Indeed, there is some seriously good advertising out there. The common elements tend to be intelligent and irreverent humour, flipping a finger to orthodoxy, and building on authentic core truths but in wildly imaginative ways, often with a surprise ending.

Then why, may I ask, hasn't this new brand of advertising been successful in reaching women? The Television Bureau of Canada says 70 percent of advertising targeted to women is virtually ignored. (There are warehouses full of other studies citing the same thing.) If you ask women, as we have, it's mostly the agency's fault. If you ask the agencies, they'll tell you their work is only as good as their client. If you ask the companies themselves, well, frankly, no one is really asking the companies.

We live in a consumer-obsessed world rife with media-based stereotypes. For women, they can range from Clairol's Herbal Essence Shampoo campaign, in which women had orgasms in a wide variety of public places while washing their hair, to Dove's "Campaign for Real Beauty," which dumps these flat-out dumb images on their head. Frankly, I can't decide which confuses me more with the Clairol campaign: (1) Did the hot water run out at home? (2) What the hell was in that shampoo? and (3) How is it possible that this inane campaign lasted for 10 years? (*Author's note:* The Herbal Essence idea was stolen from the wildly successful and iconic lunch scene in the movie *When Harry Met Sally.* The ad was unofficially riding on the coattails of the success of the movie and the almost-zeitgeist effect of this scene in particular, which people still remember. Though it made for a funny movie scene, the idea for a shampoo ad was outrageous in its stupidity and didn't transfer well to television, certainly not 10 years later when its endurance seemed to suggest that the company believed it was really talking to women.)

Our marketing expert Helen Bullingham says, "The irony is that there are so many products marketed as 'made for women'—think deodorant, house cleaners, toothpaste, laundry detergent—all purportedly created to make women's lives easier. However, the way women are portrayed in these ads is completely out of touch with reality. So what about this made-for-women myth? Do toothpaste and soap actually make my life simpler? No more than toilet paper does from a purely functional standpoint. One could surmise, then, that Proctor & Gamble, Unilever, Colgate-Palmolive aren't really gender intelligent from a product-development standpoint. So if these products aren't made to improve women's lives, why are they all being marketed to women? Because women not only do the buying, they influence the buying. They not only influence within the family, but within their enormous social network. In terms of a campaign's success, women can kill as quickly as create. And advertisers and marketers know this."

Advertising is one of the major contributors to women feeling that they aren't taken seriously. For years now, there have been machinations, teeth-gnashing, and chest-beating over the topic of women and advertising. It's been analyzed, theorized, and criticized to death with what appears to be little appreciable progress. While there are some bright lights, it speaks volumes that you can name them all without running out of breath. The women in our research tell us this: Companies aren't where *they* are, both in the metaphorical and physical sense. Companies and their advertising agencies continue to target women with hilariously outdated, flat-out incorrect, one-dimensional, stereotypical images, messages, and mediums. Here are a few things we have learned over the years:

1. Historically and, arguably, today, companies have done a deplorable job "speaking" to women. There is a stunning lack of gender-intelligent leadership around this issue. When we introduce the topic of advertising in our focus groups, it's like turning on a Bunsen burner. Is there too much bad blood between marketers and their targets? The intersection of marketers and women as their target is like a bad relationship; the only way to move forward is to have a fresh start.

2. In these times of limited resources, you need to pour big bucks into traditional media to get results. Why? Women have tuned out. Companies have to finally figure out where women are and be sure to bring along *relevant* messaging. They need to cultivate other fields and expand beyond "same-old, same-old" in order to effectively communicate with women, areas like intelligent database marketing, the Internet, community-level conversations and other, less conventional means.

3. The perfect emotional sweet spot for gender-intelligent retail brands is this: The best ads tell universal truths that don't ignore the reality that men and women look at the world in fundamentally different ways.

4. Successful advertising that actually reaches women does not happen in a vacuum. It is intrinsically tied to successful product development, which is tied to merchandising, which is tied to the store environment, which is intrinsically tied to the salespeople, which is tied to human resources, which is intrinsically tied to leadership, which needs to be intrinsically tied to gender intelligence if any of this is going to work.

WHO ARE THESE WOMEN IN BROCHURES, ON TV AND IN MAGAZINES?

There's always lots of laughter accompanying this discussion in our listening events. To net it out:

"I do not dance with mops, not even when drunk. I do not have orgasms while washing my hair, *especially* when drunk. I do not, nor have I ever, neglected to feed my children healthy food because I work outside of the home. I am not a one-dimensional cartoon character called 'Mom' because my full-time job is raising a family. I am not, nor ever will be a—shudder—soccer mom or—gasp—'yummy mummy.' I do not 'want it all,' certainly not at the same time. This is a surefire recipe for feeling even more inadequate, only to be exacerbated by my new address in the mental ward. I am not always thin and blonde. I may be chubby and chestnut. Or red-headed and Rubenesque. I hate being told I fear risk or fear money just because of my chromosomal makeup. Shampoo or toothpaste will never be in my bag of tricks when I lure a man to my lair." And on and on it goes.

We can summarize women's opinion on how well companies communicate with them by this woman's comment at one of our listening events when referring to how companies advertise: "You either don't talk to me at all, or, if you do, you talk to me like I'm a man, like I'm some hyper, strung-out superwoman, or like I'm five." Ouch.

Dr. David Long is a professor of sociology at King's University in Edmonton, Alberta, and has done some wonderful work on women and men's portrayal in mass media, including advertising. The following is his take on what we hapless consumers of mass media have to live with. As you will see, it's not just women who suffer.

MEDIATED WOMEN AND MEN

Stereo-mythical Characters in Mass Media	
Women	**Men**
1. The Meek Plain Jane • fearful about inability to attract/catch a man • possibly psychotic, possibly lovable	**1. The Reckless Geek** • logical and clear-thinking • possibly sociopathic, possibly lovable

2. The Emotionally Fragile Princess • emotionally unstable • utterly dependent	2. The Unemotional Robot • bereft of intimate emotional expression • noncommittal in relationships
3. The Talkative Busybody • dreamy and expressive • anxious and annoying	3. The Rude Pig • ignorant and unkind • forceful
4. Lusty, Coy Seductress • uses "feminine wiles" to seduce sex-starved men • manipulative and often evil	4. The Aggressive Sexual Predator • instinctual sexual drive • forceful and insatiable
5. The Nurturing Mother • pleasant and expressive • careful and co-operative	5. Competitive Successful Provider • high occupational status/social mobility • aggressive and strong
6. The Damsel in Distress • fearful and weak • dreams of her hero	6. The Courageous Hero • winner against all odds • dominant presence
7. The (Sex) Object • body parts used by men (not a whole person) • totally submissive	7. The Macho Lover • most women (and some men) want him • fully confident
8. The Saint • pure, gentle, and kind • possibly worthy of asexual veneration	8. The Omnipotent God • powerful and all-knowing • strong and fiercely independent

If you had to choose one of these stereotypes to describe yourself, you might say you weren't on the list. But Bullingham says, "Advertising builds on these overdramatized archetypes, which are based on subtle characteristics that we all have within us, and presents them as a spokesperson, in full-blown caricature, as the person who is to speak for all of us. In fact, they speak to none of us. And, further, they have the unhappy social effect of perpetuating negative stereotypes that we continually have to struggle against in other areas of our lives."

While this is a phenomenon that affects both genders, it affects women more. Our research revealed that while both women and men did not like how they were portrayed in advertising, women were much more likely to say this was something that bothered them. Most men merely shrugged, though there is a growing backlash among men about the "Fred and Barney" form of advertising that portrays men as thoughtless, brainless louts who can barely tie their own shoelaces. And as insufferable as men may find this, they aren't the ones experiencing not being taken seriously in the more global sense. Women also have toiled with being "objects of the gaze" far more often and far longer than men have.

Advertisers need to start asking themselves deeper questions.

REMEMBER WHO YOU ARE TALKING TO

- Is this communication piece inadvertently perpetuating a stereotype?

- Who may I risk offending with this ad, poster, or sales brochure? What happens if I reverse the gender in the material? Does it still ring true?

- Will my audience recognize herself (or part of herself) in this ad?

- Are the context and content of the collateral material actually relevant and credible to women?

- Who am I asking to find out? Am I expanding my sounding board beyond the agency and the internal corporate sphere?

WHAT IS THE MESSAGE YOU ARE TRYING TO GET ACROSS TO WOMEN?

Janet Kestin, the brainchild behind Dove's successful "Campaign for Real Beauty," says, "Women respond much more personally to their portrayal in advertising than men seem to. Personally, I prefer many of the ads directed to men because they make me laugh. I think women should be talked to as if they are adults with judgment. We don't need to be spoon-fed, protected, or talked down to. The old notions of 'talking to' or 'talking at' someone have been completely blown up, courtesy of the web and PVRs. Even television, the famous one-way medium, has become more interactive in its approach. Good TV invites a viewer to do or think something. TV that hasn't caught up with the new reality mostly talks to itself. Most advertising is invisible to women. Billions of dollars are spent on people not noticing you when the first job of an ad is to get noticed. This doesn't mean using silly, offensive, or irrelevant techniques to get that attention. Good work grabs interest and doesn't let go until the message is delivered and received. Is the message relevant to its consumer and is it delivered in a way that works for her? There's a wide range of ways to accomplish this."

Chris Staples is one of the principals of the Canadian ad agency Rethink. His firm recently did spots for Sobeys that were indicative of agency and company getting it right with women, which got it right for everyone. He says, "I've worked in grocery retail for 25 years and this sector has historically been one of the slowest to reflect change in the way it markets. For years, the standard formula included a weekly flyer full of specials, weekly price and item radio spots, and a few 'feel good'

TV spots featuring gooey lifestyle shots of moms serving up picture-perfect meals to tables of adoring family and friends, often accompanied by a syrupy jingle. Women, in this world, had two roles: keepers of the family purse, and keepers of the family hearth (or stove). Some retailers are still using this formula, but most have changed with the times.

"There's been a sea of change in the way Canadians treat food preparation and mealtime. Even though women still do the majority of food purchasing and preparation, more and more men are helping out in both areas. Many households no longer include children under the ages of 18—another huge change from the past. As a result, we really try to make our commercials contain more universal truths, rather than clichéd 'mom truths.'

"Take one recent spot we did for Sobeys, called 'GPS.' In this spot, we open in a vast, unnamed warehouse store where a couple are shopping with a large, empty cart. They're quite obviously lost, in disagreement about how to proceed. The woman wants to ask for directions. The man, typically, does not, mainly because he's got a gadget to save them: a GPS unit mounted on the grocery cart. At the press of a button, they realize they're at least 70 rows from where they need to go. Cut to a friendly, easy-to-shop Sobeys store and an announcer who points out that 'Grocery shopping doesn't have to be this hard.'

"The spot was effective for a couple of reasons. First, it's aimed squarely at both men and women. They are portrayed as equals, both engaged in a chore that typically would have been seen as 'women's work.' But this doesn't mean that the spot ignores differences between the sexes. Equal does not necessarily mean the same. Men view grocery shopping like all unpleasant tasks: With the right equipment and logistics, anything can be tackled. Women, on the other hand, crave human interaction and more sensible, common-sense solutions. Both men and women can see themselves in this spot and find reasons to feel both smug and embarrassed at the same time—maybe even elbowing each other on the sofa or sharing a knowing glance: 'That's just like you, honey.'" And there it is—that emotional sweet spot that we referred to earlier.

Think about Dove's pro-age versus anti-age products and advertising—"Fat or Fabulous." They have the right language, and are gutsy with visuals. The early executions of the MasterCard "Priceless" campaign were also interesting from a gender-intelligence point of view: It's not the stuff you buy, it's the experiences you live.

WHAT ARE YOU TRYING TO TELL WOMEN?

- Does your message tell women that you get how complex their life is? Is it actually relevant to the problems they are trying to solve?

- Are you speaking to them in a way that's insightful, intelligent, and engaging?

- Playful is good, but is your message denigrating to men? The women you're trying to reach may have sons and nephews, and worry about the stereotypes they'll inherit.

HOW CAN COMPANIES USE DATA WOMEN HAVE GIVEN IN A WAY THAT ACTUALLY MEANS SOMETHING?

Women provide marketers with unlimited data about their needs and wants and marketers have the opportunity to use this information strategically to improve profitability. Yet, most companies ignore this valuable source of information or use it so ineffectively that women wonder why they bother being so generous with their personal information. Imagine being a teacher. At the end of every day, the knowledge of your students is wiped clean and they retain nothing of what you have taught them. Tomorrow, you have to start again. How would that make your life? That is the life of a woman consumer today; she teaches retailers every day about her needs and wants, but many retailers don't retain this knowledge or use it to help her.

Don Peppers and Martha Rogers talk about the true one-to-one relationship in their work called *One-to-One Marketing*. In true one-to-one marketing, customers are teaching through their own buying behaviour and the merchant is learning. Over time, the merchant learns about buyer preferences and has earned the right to charge the customer a premium. The reason? The retailer is saving that customer the time and effort required to reteach another merchant.

There's a big difference between a retailer-centric environment versus a customer-centric environment, and women are remarkably adept at intuiting the difference. Bullingham believes that "The same holds true for database marketing. Women know if you are using their information to help them or help yourselves."

Here's a really basic database marketing/customer service example from a company that actually prides itself in understanding the woman consumer. Volvo is a very sophisticated company with a product most women love. The company knows women like to establish relationships with the companies they do business with. Would you be able to guess this from the following email exchange? The woman in this story is my neighbour Heidi.

From: Volvo Cars of North America, LLC
Sent: Sun 11/02/2007 12:01 PM
To: Heidi Finch
Subject: Welcome to Volvo

Dear Heidi,

Thank you for choosing Volvo. As you know, we strive to build the safest, most well-engineered cars on the road today. Your choice of Volvo confirms the human values we prize in building cars for people like you.

We want you to know of our commitment to continue to deliver the safest, most enjoyable driving experience possible. No matter what the current trends or how the industry may change, these are the core principles that have made our company a world leader.

I would like to personally welcome you to the Volvo family. You have become part of a rich tradition of putting people first, as demonstrated through our safety innovations and care for the environment.

If there's ever anything we can do, please feel absolutely free to e-mail me anytime, visit our website, or call 1-800-715-4408.

Drive Safely,
Volvo Cars of North America, LLC

- -

From: Heidi Finch
Sent: Mon 12/02/2007 8:00 AM
To: Volvo Cars of North America, LLC
Subject: Welcome to Volvo

I appreciate your note "welcoming us to the Volvo family."
I think I should mention that we just purchased our sixth Volvo and my husband and I have been driving Volvos for about
15 years. I know your note was written with all very good
intentions; however, just an FYI—to a long-time Volvo driver,
your note may make them feel like a forgotten cousin at a
family reunion.

Congratulations on your new role, Anne. It's encouraging to see Volvo put a woman in this lead position in a
market where a large percentage of the buying decision
is made by women.

Best regards,
Heidi Finch

Ouch Again.

Bullingham says, "When companies do implement customer
relationship marketing (CRM) programs, they can be self-serving
and short-term focused, offering customers discounts on new
products. The organization must make a short-term profit on
the program as a justification for its existence. But all of the data
that consumers are providing should be used for some higher
purpose, which ultimately should improve the customer's life and
give the retailer long-term strategic advantage. And since women
influence or make 80 percent of purchase decisions, it is women's
lives who ought to be improved with this knowledge."

She cites a specific example from her own life that graphi-
cally illustrates the lack of imagination in many retailers. "For
the last several years now, I have been giving my purchasing
data to a well known drug store through its loyalty program.
The short-term benefits are that I earn points that save me

money; I have to spend about $350 to save $5. But here's what I don't expect: Every now and then, I buy candy at the store for my kids. Turns out the data was used to determine who might be interested in sampling an obscure brand of licorice. So, this piece of plastic-covered licorice shows up in the mail one day, tucked inside a direct-mail piece! It was actually a little frightening, receiving food in the mail. In my mind, using data to sell me something else is a cheap loyalty shot. After four years of providing the company with data, I expect more. For example, the store should know by now that I have children, based on the fact that I have bought countless packs of kids' bandages, treats, toys, and other kid-related stuff and swiped my loyalty card every time. They could pre-empt my summer and winter stress by offering me summer health kits with suntan lotion, bug spray, and hats, and winter-relief packs with mitten warmers, lip balm, hot chocolate, and kids' gloves all bundled together. Throw in a few online codes for seasonal kids' games à la Kinder egg and maybe an online forum for moms to discuss and swap seasonal family ideas. This would actually save me time—pulling all these seasonal essentials together—and make me and my kids feel good."

There are companies that are taking full advantage of data in an intelligent way: Holt Renfrew customers get invited to premier launches and parties at the stores. They rub noses with the who's who of entertainment and design. At Addition Elle, a national ladies' clothing chain, Elite members receive regular communications and phone calls with notice of sales, discount savings for members, gifts with purchase, and information about new clothing lines in the store. When members hit a predetermined sales amount, they get $25 off their next purchase. Members continually receive relevant communications and always feel like they are in the know about sales, new merchandise, and special programs. You can tell by the merchandise in-store that Addition Elle uses their data to improve the merchandising selection to give women what they want. There is always a fantastic selection of cute, trendy, and sexy clothing for the larger-framed women. There are even larger-sized bracelets, necklaces, and rings to accessorize the outfits. Pretty much any trend out there this season is reflected and available in-store. Now, that's giving women what they want.

USING DATA IN A GENDER-INTELLIGENT WAY

- What will you do with the information? Will it be meaningful to women? They expect something authentic in return for this information, not be annoyed or harassed.

- Is your company able to go beyond base analytics and personalize your offer based on women's unique needs and situation?

- Are you rewarding your clients' loyalty in a way that has value for them? Are you using the data to solve their problems or improve their life in a meaningful way?

WHERE DO COMPANIES THINK WOMEN ARE?

When companies want to talk to women, they typically try to reach them in the most traditional of places—women's magazines, TV, and radio. We've already heard how unbelievably crowded these mediums are and women are essentially zoning out. This is why the Internet is exploding as a means to reach people in a whole new way.

You'll Find Them on the Web

The Internet, the great leveller, can give marketers an opportunity to redefine how they talk to women. It is still relatively new so marketers are more cautious about approaching it. Many retailers do so as an opportunity to start with a fresh, clean slate. Bullingham says, "The Internet gives rise to opportunities that can replace or add a new function or service. As a result, it has the opportunity to improve the lives of women. Because the medium already offers many women-oriented sites, it doesn't have the irrelevant communication baggage of television, for example."

For women, consumer power is about being informed, and the Internet is fuelling that power. The Internet ranks as a favourite source of information for women, who now constitute half the shoppers online. But you need to understand what motivates them to go online and check you out, how women actually surf the web in order to create a gender-intelligent online experience. Women and men behave differently online. Going back to Dr. Burke's research:

The Beaver and the Octopus—Online

Men	Women
<ul><li>Shop online less frequently than women</li><li>Prefer a site that allows them to custom-design products</li></ul>	<ul><li>Look at more on a company's website in the same way as they cover more territory in the physical store</li></ul>

(Continued)

▪ Are more tolerant of online advertising ▪ Express greater interest in product specs, history, and country of origin ▪ More willing to access customer service using a computer's voice or videoconferencing capabilities ▪ More interested in online and in-store product auctions ▪ More interested in viewing a map of the local retail store with product locations	▪ Find online advertising intrusive ▪ Prefer to speak to a real person when placing an order or re-questing assistance ▪ Look for a variety of features that increase shopping convenience ▪ Are more insistent than men that they be notified through email when online orders are received and shipped

Meet Our Three Web Greek Goddesses

Lucie Tanguay, marketer extraordinaire, has been my right hand in gender-based market research for years. Her often scary, analytical mind brought her to an intriguing conclusion a while back around women's use of the Internet. It appears, according to Tanguay, "When women go online, they alternate between three distinct 'need states.' It's interesting to watch them individuate or morph between the classic Greek roles of Artemis the Hunter, Demeter the Gatherer, and Hestia the Socializer. Men, on the other hand, tend to operate primarily as the Hunter."

Artemis the Hunter

Artemis is the Greek goddess of the hunt, the moon, and the natural environment. She usually surfs during the day between tasks, during short, highly focused sessions. When online women operate in this hunting mode, they are primarily *task-driven*: they want to find an answer to a specific question, solve a problem, pay a bill, book a trip. Artemis values well-organized websites with intelligent search engines that give her the information she needs in two or three clicks. She has no time to waste and gets very frustrated with pages that take forever to load, circle mazes, and dead ends. She is impatient and ruthless: She will leave your website angry and swear never to return if she doesn't quickly and easily find the information she wants.

Demeter the Gatherer

Demeter is the Greek goddess of agriculture, grain, and bread. She makes the crops grow and is responsible for the harvest and is also intimately associated with the seasons. She's a gatherer. Today's Demeter often surfs at night when the kids are asleep and her workday is done. She's looking for a longer, more relaxed Internet experience as a way to have time for herself. Online women operating in the Demeter persona are primarily *knowledge-driven*: They want to learn something new, acquire skills, or expand their knowledge base on a specific topic. Because she has superior peripheral vision and her brain is organized for multitracking, Demeter the Gatherer likes home pages that provide everything at a glance. She abhors having to scroll down a page to get a global view of a website. She is looking for useful, comprehensive information from a reliable source, and appreciates the ability to drill down on a specific topic of interest. But she needs a well-organized website free of visual clutter to do so because she hates feeling overwhelmed. Indeed, women feel the glut of online information more than men do. Although both men and women like having access to a lot of information online, 24 percent of women feel overwhelmed by it, compared to 19 percent of men.[1] Remember, when it comes to information processing, men *eliminate* while women *integrate*.

Hestia the Socializer

The third need state women display while online is that of Hestia, Greek goddess of house and home, the family and civic hearth, and the sacrificial flame. When online women operate in this need state, they are *relationship-driven*: They want to strengthen their bond with family and friends, expand their circle of friends, or learn about what other people think and do. The way they do this goes beyond email. After the events of September 11, men visited more websites to tell them about what was happening, while more women said the Internet helped them find people they needed to reach.[2] The typical user of MySpace™, which in 2006 eclipsed Google™ and Yahoo™ for the first time as the number-one visited website in the United States,[3] is a 21-year-old single woman who is interested in online friendship and logs on weekly to engage with a mixed list of mainly female "friends" who are predominantly acquaintances.[4]

Hestia the Socializer wants to share, listen, and be heard. She values features such as "Talk to an Expert," "Share with Friends," anything that provides a human touch, but make sure

---

1   Deborah Fallow, Pew Internet & American Life Project, "How Women and Men Use the Internet" (December 28, 2005).
2   Ibid.
3   htpp://www.hitwise.com
4   Mike Thelwall, University of Wolverhampton School of Computing and IT, "Social Networks, Gender and Friending: An Analysis of MySpace Member Profiles" (July 26, 2007).

it's authentic. Nothing irks her more than the lack of a quick and relevant response to her emails, or feeling that she is being probed for personal information.

Online (and, arguably, other places), men primarily operate under the Hunter need state, whereas women tend to alternate between all three: the Hunter, the Gatherer, and the Socializer, sometimes switching from one to another during the same surfing session. Bottom line? You need to please all three goddesses to become a top destination website.

The Three Goddesses—Online

	Artemis the Hunter	Demeter the Gatherer	Hestia the Socializer
Focus	Task-driven	Knowledge-driven	Relationship-driven
Turn-ons	<ul><li>Intelligent search engine</li><li>Fast and easy navigation</li><li>No unnecessary distractions</li></ul>	<ul><li>A site that's orderly and "clean"</li><li>Bright colours, beautiful pictures</li><li>Everything seen at a glance</li><li>Well categorized, with clear tabs</li><li>Rich, value-added, regularly updated content from a credible source</li></ul>	<ul><li>Family-friendly</li><li>Easy access to real people</li><li>Sharing tools</li><li>Quick and personal response to inquiries</li></ul>

(Continued)

| Turn-offs | • Pages that take five birthdays to load
 • Obscure language
 • Clicking on something and landing somewhere you didn't expect
 • Mazes and dead ends | • Visual clutter, too many words
 • Having to scroll down
 • Inconsistent positioning of tabs
 • Squinty print or colours that make it difficult to read
 • Too much action on the screen
 • Poor or inconsistent branding | • Feeling you are being probed for personal information
 • Having to create yet another log-on ID and password |

Sobeys Learns a Little Greek

In the online world, lifestyle websites are huge, with the likes of *Canadian Living*, Kraft, and The Food Network enjoying enormous popularity. For example, Kraft's "What's Cooking" loyalty program personalizes email recipes and magazine content based on known preferences. If you have little time, all you have to do on their website is enter the three primary ingredients you want to cook with that night and—presto!— there is a selection of recipes to choose from that you can whip up pretty quickly.

Sobeys knew that one of women's biggest stressors is dinner, because the dinner deadline comes every night whether you are working late, at home, travelling, on vacation, or sick in bed. With this in mind, Sobeys wants to become a top Canadian online lifestyle website destination through sobeys.com and compliments.ca.

To ensure that what they were offering was taking women seriously and was what women were looking for, Sobeys asked us to conduct research around their websites. Mauer Chiarello, Director of Corporate Brands Marketing, says, "Although we have a lot of understanding on women's grocery shopping habits, the online space was a relative unknown and we wanted to understand how to replicate the experience in-store to the online space." The research revealed that Sobeys' instincts were solid. However, it also revealed places where Sobeys could go deeper and wider.

Artemis the Hunter enjoyed using sobeys.com's powerful search engine for recipes and found it easy to find the store nearest to her home or place of work. She appreciated the fact that Sobeys acknowledged her time poverty and went the extra length to specify the store's nearest intersection. She also appreciated the ability to link the weekday meals recipes she found on compliments.ca to a shopping list.

Demeter the Gatherer loved sobeys.com's bright colours and appetizing food pictures. She was pleased with the rich information content on both sites and the detailed "how-to" sections she could consult to hone her culinary skills. She also appreciated the complete meal plans—from appetizers to dessert—that she found in the "Big Ideas" section of the Sobeys website.

Hestia the Socializer loved the human touch provided by Chef James and Chef Ryan, as well as the "Send-a-Friend" feature available on sobeys.com recipes. In addition, the fact that she could find a store or department manager's name and phone number in a couple of clicks gave her the assurance she could talk to a real person if she needed to.

Still, there was lots of room to improve the execution of both sites to better address all three goddesses' needs. To begin, we found opportunities related to layout, copy, and visuals. Demeter the Gatherer found both sites busy and wanted the ability to see everything at a glance. On the current site, she had to scroll down. Some sections were too wordy and poorly organized, and she asked for better categorization of recipes while in the "View All Recipes" mode. Meanwhile, Artemis the Hunter found her search abilities impaired by a layout that was not always intuitive, language that was sometimes rather obscure, and a few mazes and dead ends.

Applying a gender lens to both sobeys.com and compliments.ca also highlighted places for new features to help women with their meal planning and preparation challenge, address women's chronic time poverty, and support them in their role as guardian of their family's health and wellness.

As a result of the research, the design look and feel of compliments.ca has changed dramatically. A cleaner design with intuitive navigation has been incorporated, and the compliments.ca site has launched a new online-flyer format that incorporates a shopping cart function. It's a work in progress, and more is being done as we speak.

Bullingham says, "Any web strategy needs to link in with what the rest of the company is doing. For example, the *Compliments* magazine stands out from the mounds of grocery flyers we receive. It includes easy-to-make recipes with ingredients I can find at the store. It's seasonal and helps to add a bit of new zest to summer, fall, etc. It helps readers. As far as the store goes, what I appreciate about it is that I don't have to walk through a shopping mall–sized grocery store to get what I need. Another very smart thing that they did recently was this: With the neighbouring

Loblaws store having closed, Sobeys knew that some of Loblaws' customers would be shopping there and since the two store layouts were completely different, previous Loblaws customers wouldn't know where to get their regular stuff. They had staff available who would walk you right to the product category you were looking for and show you what was on sale—very effective for helping to lock in new customers."

WOMEN'S ONLINE "MUST-HAVES"

Here are some "must-haves" when designing a site that incorporates women's online styles and preferences.

Provide a seamless, tailored experience.

Build profiles, customize messages and offers, and allow the customers to use their profile to tell you what they want. Some experts say less than 20 percent of the content should be generic to all users.

Provide relevant content in understandable language.

Women are looking for trusted filters of information to help them weed through the volume of information available. Use a combination of unique elements, whether in merchandise, services, information, or related links to support what you are selling.

And remember, there's no need to impress women with big words and technical jargon.

Organize your content effectively.

Develop learning centres that provide information to help women consumers make more educated buying decisions. Come up with a way to present a sample to help them decide. Include summary documents or top-10 lists where appropriate. Women appreciate the opportunity to choose how to interact with a brand before they poke around in other areas, and they'll return for more.

Post your corporate soul.

Putting more information about who your company is and what it stands for enriches the corporate profile for the online reader. It's how your online customer gains an understanding of your organization. That information is often noticeable by its absence. We know in the automotive world, for instance, that women—more so than men—focus on environmental and safety-related information, and judge accordingly. They also evaluate your sense of corporate and employee responsibility, watch how you handle various situations, and care about what contributions you make to society. Women notice things in the periphery, such as which social causes your brand supports; if there are women on your board; and whether or not your content is written in a way that speaks to them in their language. The online realm offers much more ability to check these peripheral issues out with ease, so brands must tend to them. Include information about your company's ethics policy, community links, flextime options, or on-site child care. Pick social causes to support that reflect your women customers' concerns.

Don't waste time.

Women simply don't have any time to waste. Research has shown that the shorter the click path from the home page to the actual transaction, the more likely the customer will buy. Stick to the "eight-second, three-click rule." If it takes more than eight seconds to download a page or three clicks to get to the information desired, forget it. If there is a download or survey, indicate how long it will take and set expectations in advance. Organize searches according to how customers purchase a product (by gender and age, or by department, brand, gender, or use, depending on the industry).

Understand women's consumer behaviour.

Women tend to recycle patterns that were successful in the past, so pay attention to what is already working. Also, remember women's proclivity for internally amplifying their negative experiences. If they have one or two bad experiences on your site, they'll flee. Maximize retention by becoming the destination site. Use loyalty programs, online interactions with expert advisers, and chat rooms for like-minded individuals. Share knowledge and allow self-discovery. Maintain some level of friendly human interaction ("live" or via email) with customers through all phases of the purchasing cycle, giving them a sense of access to inside information and validation. Make sure the site makes it easy for women to refer, with pass-along devices such as printer-friendly formats and "Email-a-Friend" functionality. Include testimonials, expert reviews, awards, and seals of approval.

Be safe.

Research shows women are more concerned than men about online security and privacy. A study from Ryerson University[5] found that more than one-third of all the sites fail in this critical component of e-tailing and one-third need improvement to meet the minimum standard.

WHERE ELSE WILL YOU FIND WOMEN? IN THE COMMUNITY

In certain circumstances, it makes sense to reach women in a highly specialized and unconventional way. In cases where the product or service is complicated or provocative, entering into a direct dialogue

---

5   Shirley Dawe and Wendy Evans, with M. Denney, "Top of the E-Class: Ranking and Best Practices of Over 170 Websites." Ryerson University's Centre for the Study of Commercial Activity, 2000-04.

with women is essential. No better example of this exists than in the controversial realm of nuclear power. One of the most fascinating research projects we've undertaken was with Bruce Power, Canada's first private nuclear generating company. One of its claims to fame is that it "powers every fifth light bulb" in Ontario.

Susan Brissette, then Bruce Power's VP of corporate communications, had just reviewed a recent study prepared for the Canadian Nuclear Association that showed 58 percent of Canadian women versus 44 percent of men do not support or understand the value of nuclear. While Brissette maintains that there are critical reasons for understanding *all* stakeholders in this issue, women were of specific interest to her. She knew that women are powerful opinion stakeholders in the spheres of public policy, consumer decisions, and the family. Women's jungle telegraph is the stuff of legend. She also knew in her gut that Bruce Power could gain valuable insights into how to better communicate with the public overall if they could understand the heart of women's concerns.

CASE STUDY: BRUCE POWER

We were hired to travel across Ontario to conduct a perception audit of where women stand on nuclear power. We conducted listening events covering rural and urban centres from Ottawa to Thunder Bay, and from Toronto to Temagami.

In the groups, we explored everything: waste management, alternative energy sources, safety, conservation, industry image, and the way the industry currently communicates with the public. We discovered many things, but one really stood out: People are not benign or neutral on this topic. One of the many questions we asked was, "What's the first thing that pops into your head when you hear 'nuclear'?" The responses ranged from "death" and "The Simpsons" at one end to "cheap, clean power" at the other. While we noted an incredible variance in opinions, one thing did ring loud and clear: Women admitted their knowledge in this area was poor. This lack of knowledge, however, did not seem to preclude them from having a strong opinion. Of the many opinions stated, we noticed women held out their opinions as "truth." The participants' "truths" represented a full spectrum from "nuclear power is extremely dangerous" to "nuclear power is safe and clean." From a corporate communication perspective, this is a categorical nightmare.

The need for education was pretty evident. In an online survey that we conducted, we made the following statement: "Ontario's electricity is generated using coal, water (hydro), gas, nuclear fission, wind, and other renewable technology." A whopping 47 percent said that they needed more information before they could answer "true" or "false." In fact, out of the 400 women who participated in the research, 35 percent of respondents rated their knowledge level as 2 or lower on a scale of 0 to 10. A staggering *79 percent* rated their knowledge of nuclear power as 4 or lower.

Despite nuclear power having a reasonably safe reputation in Canada, women are still very concerned about its safety, including its effects on health and the potential for disasters. Women asked for significantly more information about (1) what is currently being done and (2) what will be done in the future to ensure that these issues are being managed effectively.

There was also distrust in the industry, which is a significant hurdle for any company attempting to reach out to specific constituency. Comments such as "Give us facts and don't spin them into marketing" and "Communicate, don't manipulate" were prevalent.

Another interesting trend emerged that you don't see as much in male-centred focus groups. The women continually asked what would be done with the results and asked if they could see the final report. They wondered if they could contact the company directly. When you ask women to engage, know that they often put a stake in the ground. From women's point of view, this is the beginning of a relationship.

Because of the research results, Brissette wanted to simply and plainly *talk* to women, face-to-face, eye to eye, heart to heart, without spin and without the chest thumping that usually accompanies this topic. We came up with a way to provide a simple, unfiltered educational forum where women from the nuclear power industry could engage in a dialogue with women public-opinion stakeholders. The concept was based on a "town hall," which reached out to women on women's terms. It included several dynamics:

1. It was not about "selling." It was about reporting research results that soundly revealed women's demand for more relevant information on nuclear power.
2. It provided an all-women forum so there would be a women-styled debate with no hesitancy in asking questions (we'll discuss ritual opposition in Chapter 9).
3. It created a professional networking opportunity with other women thought and opinion leaders.
4. It established the beginning of a relationship—good or bad—with an industry that had no direct connection to

women before. This was achieved by the ability to listen to and speak with senior women of Bruce Power on a personal and professional level. The panel shared personal stories, for example, of why they had chosen the nuclear power industry as a career and the often hilarious adventures (uniforms only in men's sizes, broom closets for change rooms as there were no women's washroom, etc.) they encountered along the way.

5. Each venue was intimate and informal. Despite the name, it never felt like a "town hall." There were never more than 30–35 guests; there was no podium, microphone, or PowerPoint presentation; the women from the company sat on sofas; and there were comfortable armchairs in the front row to draw the audience closer and put them at their ease.

6. There was a novelty factor. An all-women's event in a cool venue to talk about nuclear power complete with a chocolate fountain—now that was something that was memorable. Brissette says, "We have direct evidence that they left with a better understanding of nuclear power. Study after study has shown that the more Canadians know about nuclear power, the more favourable they feel toward the technology."

The panel of women had diverse roles, from the company's community educator to a control-room shift supervisor, the first woman in the world to receive the certification for that position and, of course, Brissette. I facilitated the sessions. The first point of order was to report on the research results and zero in on what made women mental. The three main issues were knowledge and information, safety, and alternative forms of energy.

We then opened the floor so the women could take advantage of the opportunity to pick female brains on what has traditionally been a man's world. Though it initially started as a way to report back to the research participants what we found, the forum was so successful that we branched out to include women in the general population. Brissette says the town halls have moved the needle in terms of women's perception of nuclear power. "Two things drove that change. First, the actual town halls themselves. The novelty factor for the women who attended them created something to talk about, and women love to share stories. These well-respected opinion leaders could now be opinion leaders in one more area—nuclear power. The fact that not all of them left the events as advocates for the technology was not seen to be a failure. They were powerful opinion shapers who had more accurate facts about nuclear power than they did before and maybe a different perception of the industry. Bruce Power's goal was to provide facts, build trust by putting a fresh face on the industry, and arouse women's curiosity about both sides of the issue of nuclear power."

The second thing that drove the change was that the industry woke up to women as an opinion group. It was a bit like the butterfly effect: The combination of the research and the first town hall event, which were modest compared to what the industry typically invests in opinion polling and PR, drove a significant shift in the industry. The penny dropped—women matter. The nuclear industry started looking at the gender gap and reconsidering their advertising campaigns, asking "Will this resonate with women?"

It didn't happen on its own, but Brissette can be very persuasive. Around the same time, Brissette launched a group called "Women in Nuclear (Canada)" to provide professional-development opportunities for women working in the industry, who typically make up less than a fifth of its workforce, and to provide a forum for women to educate themselves so they can better educate the public about nuclear power. Brissette says, "The industry needed to innovate and Bruce Power's gender-based research program was a catalyst. In hindsight, with social media sites like Facebook about to explode into our everyday life, this was a sound strategy. It is no longer the company who controls the message, it is the community."

The lesson here is to think outside the box, to metaphorically go where women are with relevant messaging. More often than not, you may need to talk to women directly in meaningful ways that respect their intelligence. One could safely surmise that Bruce Power never would have formulated a quality relationship with women using traditional media or online relationship management.

WHY ARE WOMAN CONSUMERS STILL HAVING THIS CONVERSATION?

The collective state of women's antipathy towards the general state of communication puts companies in a more perilous position, as it's much harder to break through the wall and actually connect. But do not mistake this as malaise or indifference. When a winning communication strategy actually breaks through women's state of coma around companies, the response is staggering.

Kestin of Dove's "Campaign for Real Beauty" fame, says, "Women are not alone in their antipathy toward advertising.

I think there's an increasing sense that advertising, in the old-fashioned sense of the word, 'doesn't relate to me and I certainly don't relate to it.' The best brand communication intersects with people in their lives. It doesn't scream at them through the screen or invade their space until they just can't take it anymore. It can be helpful (I play your online game and you give me a value-added coupon; I look at your deeper message on your website and you connect me to a community of my peers), entertaining, powerful, advocacy, informative in itself, or lead you to the information you need. When great work happens, and it can be via any medium, women come out in droves as has been the case with Dove's 'Campaign for Real Beauty.' Viewed by women as the first major brand, along with Nike, to invest in who women really are, they've spoken, supported, participated, and shopped Dove. Clearly, when it works, you enlist a huge population. But in the end, campaigns only survive if people buy the stuff companies are selling. I invest in you, you invest in me. It's the way of the capitalist world."

GENDER-INTELLIGENT SALES COMMUNICATION TOOLS

1. Start with understanding the complexity of women's lives. Women notice more than men, which figures into their assessment of your communications.

2. Make your message socially progressive versus stereotypical. Show women realistically busy yet handling the chaos with confidence and a sense of humour.

3. Step away from the conventional "product as hero" and focus on relevant human benefits, not facts and features. Show emotion.

4. Women better absorb information when it's presented in context, as used in a typical situation. Place the product within its environment, lifestyle, and feelings.

5. Build your case with strong visuals and stories. It's much easier for women to recall and recount an ad with one of these elements to anchor it.

6. Use customer information to personalize offers in a way that adds value to women's lives.

7. Follow the emerging media consumption habits of today's women.

8. Let women know about your corporate soul. Most communications miss the mark because they don't key in on women's environmental and social values. Women are more likely than men to change brands based on environmental concerns.

9. Communicate with your target group directly, not through their children.

10. Remember, women look out for family, neighbours, friends, and work associates, always conscious of things that might be relevant to someone they know and care about.

CHAPTER NINE

Controlling Your Company's PESTs:
Creating Gender-Intelligent Points of Contact

Women speak two languages—one of which is verbal.

—William Shakespeare, Poet and Dramatist

THE SALESPEOPLE PEST

A colleague of mine shared a story with me about a friend whom she described as a techno-genius, able to technically run circles around everyone. This woman worked for Hewlett-Packard for years. Lydia and her husband popped into an electronics store because she needed a PDA. The salesman saw them enter the store and zoned in. He looked at her husband and said, "Good afternoon. What can I help you with today?" Mark answered, "Oh, it's not me, it's my wife. She's looking for a PDA." Not missing a beat and not moving his eyes, the salesman replied, "Ah! Good. And what kind of PDA is she looking for?" Completely taken aback, Mark blinked, then burst out laughing. With a fuming wife beside him, you could still hear Mark howling halfway down the mall after they beat a hasty retreat.

This is the stuff of urban myth. And while the story is completely true, encountering this type of blatant, almost comic sales scenario is rare compared to the real issues. Believe it or not, it's not the neanderthal "beat over the head with a club and drag into a cave" experience that women mean when they report they aren't taken seriously. It's the more subtle and unconscious stuff that happens in the face-to-face customer experience.

For those of you who believe status quo is good enough and that you can get by on the same old, same old, there's one place that you can't hide. And even if the rest of your organization is silent on gender intelligence, your front-line salespeople are not. They are giving away your gender-intelligence level every minute of every day while they are on your sales floor. Because of retail's hyper-frenetic pace, if you aren't going forward, you're heading backward. And your staff might be the ones taking you there.

Your salespeople might be the last major encumbrance to establishing a gender-intelligent retail ecosystem. Conventional retailers continue to miss the mark here because they don't even know they have a problem. Case in point: When men complain about any type of negative retail experience, it's usually about inferior service or a product that didn't live up to their expectations. However, more than 50 percent of women in our study said they received inferior service because of their *gender*. (Guess how many men blamed their gender?) Even industry associations point to this problem. According to *The Canadian Automotive Retailing Industry Report*, "Men believe they can sell well to women and the comments we have received from consumers suggest that women have no gender preference of their salesperson. Perhaps this supports the contention that men can sell to women but few have the necessary gender sensitivity."[1] This problem will never go away

---

1   Industry Canada, *The Canadian Automotive Retailing Industry Report (2000).*

until companies start using a gender lens on sales and customer service training.

No more brilliant example of the necessity of this lens exists than this following story. We have worked with countless numbers of men in sales who admit selling to women is harder than selling to men. It goes something like this: "I'm professional, I do everything right. I give her tons of good information, I answer questions, and I listen. She gives me all the right buying cues, and I go in for the close. She walks out of my office and I never see her again."

We heard this with such frequency that we decided to dig around to see what was up. What was "up" fell smack into the realm of gender differences in communication styles. We asked how they knew that the woman prospect was so in synch with their sales presentation. The number-one answer was: "She was buying into everything I was saying. She nodded in agreement throughout the whole sales presentation. It was pretty clear she was agreeing with me. It felt like the right time to close."

And there it is, ladies and gentlemen.

For the men reading this book, please pay close attention to what follows. This piece of information will not only make you a better business person, but can dramatically improve your life at home: When a women nods her head, it's a listening cue: "Go on . . . I'm listening . . ." In fact, it's a pretty safe bet that it's not a sign of agreement at all. Women are actually quite capable of nodding their head in what appears to be agreement, yet really be thinking, "You just might be the biggest goof I have ever met . . ."

With men, head nodding is simple to read—yes or no. While most of these men are good salespeople, they were way off in terms of understanding women's readiness to close. They have misunderstood a classic feminine communication ritual—nodding as an indication of active listening.

So imagine my reaction while sitting in a sales training room one day. I was hired by Toyota to do a gender-based audit on a new-hire training session. I could barely contain myself when the well-intentioned trainer said, and I quote, "As you go through the process and you present paperwork, the client is nodding. That's the goal. Why? What are you getting the client to do? *Agree with you!*"

Well, no actually. Women continually complain that many men who sell to them are too aggressive and hard sell. It's a safe bet this is part of the reason. Men interpret head nodding as a buying signal and jump in to close before that all-too-important relationship has been established.

This head-nodding ritual can create havoc for women in other ways. A senior banker once told me her experience as an account manager. She'd listen intently, nodding, to small business owners explaining why the bank needed to fund their entrepreneurial dream. She noticed that men often reacted with more surprise and anger at being declined than the women did. At first, she thought it was merely an ego thing, but then realized she may have inadvertently given the impression of buying into their sales pitch by nodding throughout the conversation.

This is one small example of why training needs to be hauled through a gender lens. Well-intentioned companies provide tons of information through every conceivable channel without first figuring out how to get through to women. They don't get the most important source of information right: the sales force.

GENDER-BASED CULTURES

Believe it or not, as there are with different ethnic groups, there is also a gender-based "culture." In *Talking from 9 to 5: Women and Men in the Workplace, Language, Sex, and Power* (HarperCollins, 1995), Deborah Tannen examined how women and men talk and work in the workplace. It appears we have two different cultures that are manifested in the types of communication rituals that we use. It is in our different gender cultures where we learn our "conversational rituals." These rituals are learned from the children we play with, who are often the same sex. Consequently, when we talk to the other sex, and if the conversational rituals we have learned are not shared, we tend to interpret them literally. When we do this, we can end up completely misinterpreting the speaker's intentions and abilities.[2] There are two areas where these different communication styles are known to particularly manifest: in a sales situation and in personal relationship.

Unless a company gets this right, no amount of women-friendly anything—no women's conferences, baby change tables, websites, women salespeople, women-centred advertising or marketing—no matter how expensive, will change one immutable fact: The whole thing can implode the minute a woman consumer sets foot in your establishment and turns to face the salesperson.

---

2   Deborah Tannen, *Talking from 9 to 5: Women and Men in the Workplace Language, Sex and Power*, Avon Books, New York, 1995

PROTECTING YOUR PEOPLE INVESTMENT

More than any other channel of information distribution, the face-to-face experience in the store is often the black hole for companies when dealing with women consumers. The retail industry's biggest operational cost is salaries. When there is consumer pressure to drive down pricing, the sales force usually takes the hit. This becomes a downward cycle, as fewer sales staff generally equals fewer floor staff. Organizations with a high staffing ratio and inherent gender-intelligent cultures tend to be rewarded with strong sales to support the staffing—for example, Mountain Equipment Co-op, $1,200/square foot; Lululemon, $1,400/square foot; and the ridiculous Apple Store's total of $4,300/square foot. Compare this to the average retailer with $800–$900/square foot.

Salespeople are critical to retail operations because employees are one way competitors can differentiate themselves from one another to gain market share. As Sean says, "It's hard to do anything about finding parking or the mall being too crowded, but there is something we can do about the salespeople. At the end of the day, they have to be as multidimensional as women consumers themselves are. A salesperson is an engager, an expediter, and an educator. More than anything, they have to be authentic, but they have to have a finely tuned radar so they can adjust their sales process 'frequency' depending on whether they are dealing with a woman or a man."

To that end, salespeople need to have a sense of how women and men are different. Rest assured however, that most good salespeople, certainly at a subconscious level, already know most of this. Your job is to get this intuitive stuff out of their heads and put into conscious daily practice.

The Sales Cycle: The Beaver and The Octopus

Men are often described as achievement-oriented—they are driven to accomplish external goals, achieve success, and be assertive, independent, and self-oriented. Women are affiliation-oriented—they are concerned with people's feelings, seek approval from others, want to create nurturing relationships, and strive to maintain interpersonal balance. Typically, women want to get along, while men want to get ahead. This is an incredibly condensed version of a warehouse full of academic research on gender differences. These particular characteristics are of interest because they have considerable impact on interpersonal interaction—in other words, the sales process.

Men Buy, Women Shop

In a 2008 study titled "Men Buy, Women Shop," researchers at Wharton's Jay H. Baker Retail Initiative and the Verde Group say women's role as caregivers persists even as women's professional responsibilities mount. This and the other 4,000 reasons we've previously discussed are why women have more acute shopping awareness and higher expectations. On the other hand, after generations of relying on women to shop effectively for them, many men's interest in shopping has atrophied.

According to Wharton marketing professor Stephen J. Hoch, shopping behaviour mirrors gender differences throughout many aspects of life. "Women think of shopping in an interpersonal, human fashion and men treat it as more instrumental. It's a job to get done," he says. "Communication is critical to reaching women shoppers. Sales associates must be trained to recognize and react to shoppers' cues."

As in our own research, "Men Buy, Women Shop" found that women are more likely than men to experience problems while shopping, with women over age 40 reporting more problems than men in the same age group. For women, "lack of help when needed" is the top problem (29 percent). It is also the likeliest reason why stores lose the business of women shoppers. Men, however, ranked "difficulty in finding parking close to the store's entrance" as their number-one problem (also 29 percent).

Feeling Important Versus Checking Out Fast

According to the study, men want a salesperson to help get them through the checkout quickly. For women, store loyalty is related to how well the salesperson knows the products and the store, and can create a seamless experience that includes figuring out what best suits their needs. Women shoppers also value being made to feel important.

In a telling interview with researchers, a woman in the 18–35 age bracket described the employees in her favourite store: "The sales associates are always great. They always show me different styles. They will show me something new that's come in." Meanwhile, a man in the same age bracket said this: "I haven't had much interaction with most salespeople. I don't really need them as long as they're at the checkout."

When asked what problem would make respondents so angry they would never return to a store, women cited employees who "acted like you were intruding on their time or their own conversations." Men were most miffed by employees who were "lazy, i.e., would not check for additional stock or take you to the item you were looking for."

When it comes to the retail experience, men and women both go into the store to buy something, but women want more interaction and more eye contact. Men want quick answers, while women look for support and collaboration in the buying process. It is important to point out that this is not all women and men. I am usually pressed for time and, more often than not, behave like a man when shopping. However, these studies refer to general trends and while there are clearly exceptions, most women and men tend to fall neatly into these categories.

The Beaver and the Octopus Talk to Each Other

Body Language

Another big communication issue that ranks right up there with that head-nodding thing is the often-lamented "You're not listening to me" phenomenon. Men are surprised at the frequency with which they hear this refrain. One day, I told a male insurance agent I felt he wasn't listening to me. He was shocked and then proceeded to repeat the gist of all I'd said. Puzzled, I couldn't shake the impression that he hadn't been paying attention. I began to recognize that the cause may have been nothing more than his body language—the way he positioned his body and directed his gaze. He rarely looked at me. He was always looking down and taking notes.

Tannen says this is a common male ritual in communicating. Her research shows that men can be uncomfortable with direct eye contact, perceiving it as a challenge from someone of the same sex or as flirtation if made by the opposite sex. Women, on the other hand, don't view it in that light and will often go out of their way to ensure eye contact is made.

It's good to role-play this in sales training exercises. Think of yourself as a salesperson during a client's visit. Was there direct eye contact and how did it make you feel? Are you sitting or standing facing each other directly, at angles, or side by side? How close or far apart feels right? Think of the times you have been accused of not listening when you heard every word, or when you felt you weren't being listened to. Could your body language have played a role? What was the other person's position or posture?

Ritual Opposition

I can't count the number of meetings I've been to where men appear to be beating the crap out of each other, then go off for a friendly game of squash. This baffles most women. We're taught to, at all costs, maintain an appearance of equality by avoiding boasting, downplaying our own accomplishments, or being sure to include others by asking for their opinion. Tannen's research shows that conversational rituals common among men, in fact, often involve opposition that is not meant literally. This includes banter, teasing, or discussing an idea by playing devil's advocate.

Playing devil's advocate can be one of the most effective ways to test the validity of ideas. But, as Tannen says, it's "a classic area where, if not shared, it can be construed as a literal attack." It's not uncommon for a man's first response to be 18 reasons why something is a bad idea, but in fact it's his way of processing the information. It's a form of elimination.

Many women who work in sales report that men often challenge their recommendations. Consequently, the women believed the men were attempting to undermine their "expert" status. In fact, the men were likely expecting the women to push right back and are thrown off when women back down.

In selling to mixed-gender couples, just because the man may be more vocal or dominant in the process does not necessarily mean he is the decision maker. It is often communication rituals that create the impression. Remember, women control 80 percent of the consumer dollar spent. The most hesitant, apologetic-sounding women may be the hardest to close, and the most direct and abrupt men may buy in during the first appointment.

Communication rituals can create an impression that isn't accurate. Tannen explains: "If rituals are not shared, what you say may be taken literally. Things like using verbal opposition to explore an idea can be construed as a literal attack. A playful insult can be taken as a literal one. An expression of sympathy can sound like a put-down. An expression of concern may be regarded as an apology. The missed opportunities lie in not recognizing and interpreting how men and women do business differently."

Gender Differences in Negotiation

Sociological studies indicate that women are taught to please as many people as possible, an attitude that seems weak to male negotiators. Based on the language of the male business model, women's negotiating style isn't considered as effective as men's style. In *Is It Her Voice or Her Place That Makes a Difference? A Consideration of Gender Issues in Negotiations* (Industrial Relations

Centre, Queen's University, 1992), Deborah Kolb notes that both men and women are taking more active roles in the traditional domains of each other, giving rise to gender questions. Here are the highlights of her research:

- For men, the primary matters to be dealt with are the substantive issues. For women, the quality of the relationship is most important, and they look for agreements that enhance relationships. In other words, women look for a win/win rather than a win-lose outcome.
- Women see negotiation as a part of an ongoing relationship with a past and a future.
- Women often learn through dialogue—a sharing of concerns and ideas—rather than through challenge and debate.
- Because a woman's status in negotiations is not automatically assured, she often has to be tough and aggressive to establish her place.
- Women are generally expected to be passive, compliant, non-aggressive, non-competitive, and accommodating, and to attend to the social and emotional needs of those present.
- Men and women often find that different meanings are attached to their behaviour, even when they say or do the same thing. For example, aggressive women are thought of negatively (ever heard the terms "ball breaker" or "man in a skirt"?), but aggressiveness is admired in men.

This is not about men learning to talk or negotiate like women and vice versa, but we have seen first-hand what can happen when people are merely enlightened to the fact that there are differences.

Incorrect assumptions diminish, communication pathways open up, and success rates in closing business increase.

The Power of a Simple Word: Gender-Neutral Language

A complex idea or image can be created merely by uttering a single word. Individual words can pack a lot of power because they can create very specific visual images. This is a little exercise from our training that we'll use to illustrate. We ask the group to reply "male" or "female" spontaneously when we say specific words.

"What do you think of when you hear the word 'wimp'?"
The unanimous answer is invariably "male."
"Battleaxe?"
"Female" is always the answer.

Research, as well as our little exercise, shows that we often think in pictures and that there is strong gender identification with our choice of words. So if people react so strongly to apparently non-gendered words like "wimp" and "battleaxe," what about words that are strongly gendered?

We then ask a true-or-false question: "People assume that words such as 'mankind' and 'he' apply to both sexes." Most people reply "true." Historically, and even today, terms such as "mankind," "man," and "he" are supposed to be generic and are presumed to include both men and women, but research shows that this isn't really the case. Studies with elementary, secondary, and college students show that when the term "man" is used, people envision males even when the content implies both men and women.

Tips on Gender-Inclusive Language

Look at the language of your company and begin to make changes to some of the simple things, such as using gender-neutral words or "her/she" pronouns versus the common "he/him/it." Make this a part of your sales training program as well as in all your communications. This is a gradual change—don't move from one extreme to another.

Here are some tips that we've gathered along the way.

- The word "man" as a generic term to describe men and women, or sometimes women alone, is inaccurate, offensive to some, and unnecessary when you can use words such as "people," "humans," "human beings," and "individuals."
- Eliminate the pronouns "he," "him," and "his": Use "The customer wants knowledgeable salespeople" or "Customers want their salespeople knowledgeable" instead of "The customer wants his sales representative to be knowledgeable." As a last resort, use "he or she" and "his or her."
- Avoid such terms as "manpower," "the common man," "man hours," and "man on the street." (But don't carry this to extremes by avoiding such terms as "boycott" and "manufactured," which have different roots.) Avoid "manned," as in "the store is manned by part-time workers tonight." "Staffed" will do just fine, thank you.
- Where appropriate, use neutral terms. For "man-made," use "engineered," "manufactured," "artificial," "custom-made," "handmade," etc. Use "police officer" instead of "policeman," "firefighter" instead of "fireman," "sales representative" instead of "salesman," and "letter carrier" instead

of "postman." Use generic terms for occupations, such as "camera operator," "dairy worker," "cleaner," "room attendant," "housekeeper," "bartender," and "bar worker."

- Avoid female suffixes such as -*ess* at all costs. Terms such as "manager," "author," and "waiter" cover both sexes.
- If gender is not relevant, don't point it out. We are way past mentioning "male nurse" and "woman doctor."
- You're safe being gender-specific when referring to a specific person with terms such as "spokesman" or "spokeswoman." The suffix -*person* is acceptable, but use it sparingly. "Chair" is fine.
- Refer to "husband and wife," not "man and wife." Speak of a "man and a girl" only if the girl is under 16. When referring to females aged 16 or 17, say "young woman." My dear 80-year-old friend, Ruth, thinks that those under 16 and those over 70 should all be called "girl."
- Watch for traditional expressions such as "old wives' tales." Find a substitute, such as "superstition" or "popular misconception."
- Be wary of sports and military terms. There is a preponderance of sports and military metaphors in the business world: "the front line," "making a killing," "penetrating the market," "team player," "the whole nine yards," "step to the plate," "playing in the big leagues," "ballpark figure," "getting down to the short strokes." The key is to use a mix of topics and metaphors, although not in the same paragraph. Constantly talking about "a targeted marketing campaign" or "fighting in the corners" will not motivate people who function by building relationships rather than by competing.

THE OCTOPUS AND THE BEAVER GO SHOPPING: REPRISED

The following is a sketch of how a man and a woman might approach a similar shopping "mission." By no means is this to reflect all men and all women. My husband couldn't give a hoot if he looked stupid in front of a salesperson and would be no more inclined to buy a pair of skis because his buddy said they were "the best" than to fly to the moon. (But his four brothers would . . .)

The idea here is to get a "visual glimpse" of the motivation and process for a women and a man when they walk into a store. Take note of the duration of their shopping experience, the way they move through the shopping environment, the questions they ask, and what they consider in order to make a decision. The stuff in italics reflects some of the gender-specific behaviours and thoughts.

Meet Michael and Joanne.

MEN: information-eliminators, decisions based on a limited number of cues like price or third-party recommendation, position dictates, personal excellence, beat/win, independent, detached, linear, direct, devil's advocate, competition, hierarchy, report

Michael has decided he needs new skis after talking with a colleague at work. His work buddy John was waxing poetic about how his new skis were vastly superior to the old ones he had, the ones Michael *was embarrassed* to say he owns. On his lunch hour, he walks over to a nearby store to take a look.

12:33 p.m. Michael walks into the store and notices a mannequin with a pack that allows you to attach a snowboard. Michael doesn't snowboard, but notes the *feature is pretty cool.*

12:34 p.m. Michael can't see the ski department immediately, but he *walks around* for a minute until he finds it.

12:35 p.m. He sees a salesperson, but walks by him, *zeroing* in on the skis. While he's looking at them, he's thinking, "These are what I want, I think. I'm pretty sure, I think." Michael gulps as the salesperson approaches. He looks pretty hardcore. Michael starts to worry that he's going to look like an idiot in front of this guy. He takes a deep breath and thinks, "Buddy John bloody better well know what he's talking about."

Michael asks, "Why is this ski more expensive than this one? *Is it better?*"

The salesperson replies, "The cost of the ski doesn't always mean that the ski is better. It depends on what you need. Why don't we start with where you like to ski the most and go from there . . ."

Michael then engages in a process of *eliminating* variables is order to narrow down his choice. His process is heavily influenced by *status* both in his original decision to buy the skis and in his questions with the salesperson.

WOMEN: information integrators, decisions based on a wide variety of cues, level the playing field, personal excellence, connected, interdependent, multi-level thinkers, emotion, encourage, common ground, community, talk, create rapport

Joanne has *several errands* to do downtown. She has waited until after the lunch rush because the stores will be less busy and it will be easier to *get help* and hopefully find parking.

1:35 p.m. She notices a sporting goods store because she's been *researching* getting a new pair of skis. She's worried her old pair is just *not as safe* as some of the new technology that's now available. She remembers that she needs to look for new ski goggles for her older son, who lost his on his last trip. Might as well look at ski socks. She noticed Michael's socks were a little worn the last time she did the laundry.

1:37 p.m. She sees the display several feet inside the store as she walks in. There's a pack with an unusually designed pocket that makes it really *convenient* to access what you need. "I wonder if it would actually fit me?" she muses as she walks by.

1:38 p.m. She sees a customer service desk to her right and notices some other employees a bit farther away in the clothing section. She can't see the skis so she immediately *goes to the service desk* to ask for directions to the department. Then to the washroom, always a top priority.

1:46 p.m. She was thrilled that the washrooms were clean. She also takes note of the hands-free features so that you didn't feel like you had to wash your hands every time you touched something. On to shopping . . .

1:48 p.m. Joanne scans the store, looking for the ski section. She *notices the event board* for upcoming in-store seminars on getting outside with your family; *sees the signs for the items on sale; notices the signs in the corner; briefly notices a staff member* who appears to be really listening to a customer. Finally she sees the snowsports sign and heads in that direction.

1:49 p.m. Spotting a salesperson, she walks straight and says, "I need help . . ."

1:50 p.m. Peter, a little startled by the direct question but quickly catching up, asks, "Sure, how may I help you today?" Joanne *notices Peter's friendly and casual demeanour,* but also notes he appears competent and polite. He's wearing the wildest shoes she's ever seen.

"Well," says Joanne, "I am looking for a new pair of skis. My current ones are a few years old and I am *interested in understanding* some of the new technology that I have been reading about. Parabolic skis allow you to use a shorter ski, but I don't really understand how this is better or why I should replace my old ones." Peter responds, "Good question and why don't I start there . . ."

Joanne has a much more conscious and "professional" approach to her shopping mission. She also notices and absorbs more of the environment around her. She's integrating all that is going on around her. While what her peers use is important, her selection process is more complex.

At MEC, Sean sees this behaviour repeated constantly. "Men will come in, identify a product and say, 'I want this product because that is what my peers have . . .' Men will rarely move on to any other options. Women, on the other hand, say, "This is what my peers have. I want to hear from you (the salesperson) why they are choosing that product.' Women will consider the salesperson's information and combine it with their own knowledge. They may make a choice similar to their peers, but they are equally as likely to consider other possibilities."

CREATING A RETAIL CULTURE CHANGE THAT OUTLASTS EMPLOYEES

A Gender-Intelligent Sales Force Requires Gender-Intelligent Leadership

For your salespeople to become gender intelligent, the top needs to get this. (See the theme developing here . . .?) Front-line people typically have a very specific box within which they are permitted to operate, but if you haven't changed the parameters of that box before you ask them to address the consumer differently, it won't take hold. A band-aid approach will not work. Leaders can say, "You guys just need to talk differently to these people," but if they themselves haven't really internalized what this means, a lot of resources get wasted.

It's a top-down structure in retail, so it's not rocket science. There is the core—the executive team—and if you're a national organization, there will be some version of regional supervision. Store managers need to know in very simple terms what the organization is doing to create and maintain a gender-intelligent environment. They need to know how, in very practical terms, this can be manifested at the store level and at the consumer level. Most importantly, you need to answer the question "What's in it for them as a store manager?" What incentives will the organization offer managers in the process of achieving a more gender-intelligent culture? What are the compensation structures and how do they measure results in terms of supporting gender-intelligent behaviour? This is crucial to ensuring that the company continues to drive the right behaviour.

Sounds pretty simple, but make sure your rewards and incentives support gender-intelligent behaviour. The challenge is not just looking for the short-term spike in sales but establishing a long-term connection/relationship with the woman consumer. You need to measure carefully because the people who may be successful in helping to make the culture shift may not be getting the rewards that they should be.

When you are looking for new staff, you should have a different blueprint for the kind of people you need in the organization. If there are holdouts in your organization who are responsible for recruiting but aren't adapting to change, things will pretty much stay the same. One thing is for sure. The all-too-common approach (especially in conventional industries) of simply hiring more women won't get you far, either.

Bring On the Women!

Industry research from a variety of sources, including our own, makes it pretty clear that women don't care about the gender of their salespeople. However—and it is a big however—this assumes that the salesperson has some inkling of gender intelligence.

It's important to understand that creating a gender-intelligent sales force isn't about recruiting women first or in isolation. It's about creating an environment where women will not only want to come and work, but also to stay and progress. It's acknowledging the need for change, dealing with the attitudinal barriers, and recruiting wisely. It's fostering a gender-inclusive atmosphere that stems from having people who have an open and responsive world view in critical roles. Combine all this with proper insight of women's consumer reality and your workplace will be one where women will intuitively want to do business. And remember our mantra: If you make it women-friendly, you make it everybody-friendly.

As discussed in Chapter 4, if, in concert with recruitment efforts, companies don't examine the gender messages in their internal processes—what gets rewarded, who gets promoted, what image is acceptable, how decisions get made—there is an increased chance that women recruited into the environment will not be as effective as they could be. Many may leave, not because they didn't have what it takes, but because they don't find the environment a comfortable place in which they could be successful. Put more directly, when the organization has not reviewed the organizational processes, structures, and practices—including evaluation and reward systems, line management training and support, and internal communication practices—there will undoubtedly be a credibility gap. What may be presented as a big shift in the company's strategy and direction can create an expectation of consistency in the message and the actual day-to-day experience. If the cultural experience does not ring true for a new employee hired as part of a new change initiative, people will leave or, potentially worse, shut down their initial enthusiasm and become complacent but stay. Underperformance and high turnover are costly in themselves, but other costs are just as real and affect corporate reputation and inability to get a wider gender- or diversity-based world view.

We have spent many years training sales forces only to see much of that good work evaporate. Sales turnover is high, but, more to the point, company ecosystems didn't have the internal culture in place that supported the necessary behaviour change required. This is why an organizationwide gender-lens concept is much more effective. Women's and men's different styles and needs are built in throughout the corporate ecosystem from the get-go.

In my experience, I've found that many women need a gender-awareness primer as much as men do. As we previously discussed, in most corporations, male-style behaviour is the norm and is overtly or covertly rewarded. To succeed, women must assimilate into that environment. It's so much more complex than simply having more women in the business.

Women and Men in the Workplace

	Men	Women
How do we bond?	• games and tasks	• talk
What are the reasons we talk?	• to report	• to create rapport
What is our work style?	• position dictates	• level the playing field
How do we compete?	• personal excellence	• personal excellence
How do we like to appear to others?	• beat/win	• connected
How do we think?	• detached	• interdependent
How do we express ourselves?	• independent	• multi-level thinkers
What is the best way to elicit opinions?	• linear	• feelings
How do we achieve results?	• beliefs	• politely
	• directly	• encourage
	• ask to state	• common ground
	• devil's advocate	• rapport
	• competition	
	• hierarchy	

How Do You Support This Level of Culture Change?

There are several things you can do to anchor what is necessary to create and anchor a gender-intelligent sales force.

Revise the Interview Process

Ideally, you have to find a way to screen for an awareness of gender intelligence or at least an openness to adopting that approach, and then find ways to train and reinforce it once people are hired. A good human resources department can help to design the interviewing process that will target a few key example-based questions related to diversity, picking up on the cues of women consumers, their interest in trying new approaches, and other examples that will most closely mirror the kind of openness you are looking for. Any successful organizational implementation will include a shift in metrics, and reward and recognition systems that supports the culture change-efforts.

In retail, senior management sets the tone, but the front-line managers are the key influencers on a customer's experience. This is a key group if you want to influence the overall experience and create a good place in the recruitment process to insert a gender lens. Ask interviewees about their experiences in serving women or what they would do to help improve the business for women. Look for a general understanding of gender-based consumer issues. Probe to see if they have any awareness of consumer-based gender differences (integrators versus eliminators) and ask them how they might present information differently to women and men. Are they experienced at solution-based selling? Do they interact with customers or do they interact with the product? Are they well-versed in the health, family, and community benefits and values of products?

Watch for warning signs such as comments like, "I wouldn't do anything differently" or descriptions of changes that are only superficial in nature. These warning signs indicate a lack of awareness of the customer base and before you know it, you'll be right back at the conventional retailer stage. Frankly, if your company hires people who fall into this category, then your organization is not ready to make the change.

Examine Women's Sales Experience

Try replaying call centre calls with women or ask customers' permission to tape interactions. Listen to a few different examples of your own consumers calling in, asking questions, trying to get help, trying to figure out how to put something together, or trying to manoeuvre their way through the product or service your company is offering. Then stand back and say, "So how did we do?" "What do you think they were really looking for?" "What did we miss?" "What would we do differently?" "What is she telling us?" "Did we meet her need?" This experience can give people an opportunity to change their own behaviour to better address consumers' needs in a gender-intelligent way.

It's the same drill in the store/office environment, but you need to be more creative in how to get these answers. In a store or office, this is much harder to do. Employees and customers balk at their conversations being recorded, although some retailers in the US are beginning to implement this practice. It's much more appropriate to approach this through peer support, role-playing, and mystery shopping. Team meetings are an ideal opportunity where role-playing can be used to help people anticipate consumer needs and objections, and handle difficult situations. One of the techniques we use is making video documentaries of women shoppers in a store environment. It's a bit different from mystery shopping, as it provides a broad view of the retail environment.

Encourage Gender-Intelligent Creativity

Another thing you can do is look at how you merchandise the store. Are you encouraging staff creativity in using their gender lens? They should be encouraged to try different approaches to making the store more women-friendly. Create incentives for activities such as a display of the month. Look at store-level promotions. Try a "before" and "after" in terms of performance once a gender lens was used. Make sure that the rules of the organization are not stifling initiative. Are there rules that will prevent your staff from implementing what you're asking for? For example, how you ask staff to dress; how you ask them to answer the phone; and what you expect them to count, track, or report on will drive or reinforce particular behaviours. You have to decide which behaviours need to be reinforced, and which should be de-emphasized. Do people still get in trouble for not putting the sandpaper beside the paintbrushes?

Eliminating this "people" PEST is key to establishing a gender-intelligent retail ecosystem because it's where your company "makes it real" for women consumers. It's as simple as this: Your sales staff can be either a proud beacon or an embarrassing landmark in your company's gender-intelligence landscape.

CHAPTER TEN

Mountain Equipment Co-op:
The Organic Standard

Climb like a girl. Pee like a guy.

—Julie Haas, Climber, Neuroscientist, Harvard University

THE ORGANIC STANDARD RETAILER

The "gold standard" was traditionally a way to express excellence in business. We've offered a bookload of reasons why, in today's world, this standard should morph to an organic standard. It's a far more effective means and mindset to capture the levels of excellence that your customers are looking for.

To recap: The organic standard company is one that has become evolved enough that diversity is intrinsic to everything it does. There is strong representation of women decision makers throughout the hierarchy of the organization. This awareness is translated to women consumers by the sophisticated use of language and images that demonstrate the company's understanding of how women receive and process information and make decisions. They also have a strong corporate social responsibility orientation to their business (corporate soul). They create an experience that *intelligently* recognizes gender differences.

There is a small Canadian company that has held off much larger competitors and has "owned its space" in the outdoor sporting goods world for 37 years now—Mountain Equipment Co-op

(MEC). It's grown from a kernel of an idea literally hatched on a mountaintop in a storm-bound tent into the organic standard of an organization that lives its values.

MOUNTAIN EQUIPMENT CO-OP—"IT'S ABOUT THE JOURNEY . . ."

Mountain Equipment Co-op is Canada's leading retailer of outdoor clothing and equipment, providing quality products and services for activities like hiking, climbing, cycling, and skiing. Established in 1971, MEC has more than 2.5 million members throughout Canada and around the world. They were used as a case study in my last book and remain today as one of the best examples of gender-intelligent retailing. In a lot of ways MEC is quirky and unconventional, but its business results are anything but.

MEC has 12 stores across Canada and currently enjoys a 50 percent market share of the Canadian outdoor specialty retail category. Their current revenues are a quarter billion in annual sales and they currently have no national competitors in the same retail space, although many have tried. The company's raison d'être is to provide outdoor gear affordable enough that there's still money left over to go out and play. MEC has grown into one of Canada's strongest brands with a leading-edge retail business.

MEC has much to be proud of. In 2008, it was recognized by the Conference Board of Canada as one the best-governed companies in Canada. It was selected the most sustainable retailer in Canada by *Report on Business*. While this organization's corporate values are unquestioned, what draws little attention is that this is a lean, mean retail machine that performs at the top of its industry in Canada.

Until 1997, MEC had hit the ceiling in terms of growth. In 1994, the ratio of men to women members was 70/30. Since 2007, it has evened out at 50/50, with female membership increasing at a faster rate than male membership. There were 1 million members in 1994 and today the company boasts 2.7 million. As this book went to the publisher, MEC had just completed its most successful year ever in terms of financial performance, while at the same time committing 1 percent of revenues to environmental education, advocacy, and wilderness preservation.

So what makes this organization tick? What's in their DNA that makes them who they are? And what do they do that makes them our vendor of choice for women consumers? Here is the story of this organic and transformative retailer.

An Unconventional Beginning

The structure of Mountain Equipment Co-op is a not-for-profit retail co-operative, one of the world's largest. The founders were a group of young, idealistic university students, with the first stores running on volunteer labour, a bit of prayer, and a lot of hope from a business point of view. This volunteer aspect still remains with their lay board, which is elected from its membership. It's interesting to note that MEC is one Canada's largest democratic organizations, actually bigger than most of the provinces. Since its start-up, MEC was to be an organization with a strong sense of values, one of which was that you have to be a co-operative member in order to shop at the store. A lifetime membership costs $5, the same as it did in 1971.

Every member is a shareholder, and the shareholder's value is based on his or her total value of purchases at MEC over the lifetime of the membership. MEC's evolution into organic retailing is credited with increasing to 50 percent the amount of company shareholders that are women, guaranteeing them a voice in all of MEC's endeavours. The co-operative roots of this organization have created a model built on consensus building, listening from the ground up rather than directing from the top down. Every woman walking in the door is not only a potential prospect or customer, she is a potential owner of the business.

DETERMINE YOUR COMPANY'S ECOSYSTEM

MEC drives me crazy sometimes. No matter who I talk to there— Sean, the CEO, product developers—it doesn't matter, as they always sing from the same song sheet: "We have a long way to go in serving women consumers' needs properly." The humility in this organization is a vast departure from the usual bluster and ego that I often run into. MEC gets something few other companies get: This work is never finished and will always continue to evolve.

Being a gender-intelligent company is not something they would articulate as one person's decision or even a conscious strategy. Like the transitional farmer, you don't always know *precisely* how things will turn out, but you just feel it is the right thing to do. For MEC, adopting a gender-intelligent retail ecosystem was more about gut intuition. As former CEO Peter Robinson said, "We needed to adapt to a changing economic environment and we needed to do it in such a way that we retained existing members as well as attract new ones, and all the while staying true to our values."

For the first 30 years of MEC's life, the majority of the apparel was unisex with little in the way of gendering—not unusual for the industry, but definitely the bane of one of MEC's buyers, Anne Gillespie. Gillespie (now a consultant helping companies convert to organic cotton in apparel production) was the company's footwear buyer for many years, but had just taken over the apparel lines. MEC produced mostly private label product, so Gillespie was determined to create a better apparel lineup for women. At the same time, she undertook transitioning MEC's clothing product to 100 percent organic cotton, one of the first Canadian retailers to do so.

Then Sean got in the mix and decided to take Anne's work to a whole new level—the store itself. The stores didn't even have designated areas for men's and women's apparel. (It's an outdoor thing.) At that time, most of the clothes they sold were unisex. Sean explains: "Really the idea came out of a brainstorming session with a colleague, a great retailer and a mentor, Steven Cross. We were tossing around ideas for the Toronto store layout for the spring/summer season. There was a lot of new product arriving for women, and the way we traditionally operated wasn't really working. It started with a remarkably simple idea: Why not just separate the two apparel areas and create a staff team to look after each of them?

"By no means is this a radical change for most retailers, but for us this was huge, and it made everyone nervous. I remember presenting it to the store managers and being heckled down by some for daring to break away from the way things are done. Our VP at the time, Bob Matheson, although not wild about the idea, trusted me enough to let me have a go at it, though he was pretty clear he wasn't going to bail me out if it didn't work.

"Although I was given this autonomy, which is pretty unusual for a store manager, there were a lot of things I had to commit to. The big one was that it couldn't create extra work for my colleagues and management. I had to get it up and running fast—like in 10 days—and, if it didn't work, it would come down just as quickly. There could be no additional costs to the organization, and I had to manage the costs within my existing operating budget. I had to create a single line of communication to our head office, despite having two floor managers for apparel (one for women's and kids' and another for men's). Head office wanted communication from only one person from the store.

"We also needed to adapt at the store end and that was not easy, either. My floor managers were two guys and their teams were not set up to handle women's apparel. In fact, we were one of the few women's apparel stores with a primarily male staff. To their credit, we never once received negative feedback from our members. Today our teams are more balanced, but we do not assign staff based on gender. It's based on outdoor and product knowledge.

"So here I am, caught in the middle. I have company management on one side, who were not particularly keen on the idea, and my direct reports on the other, who weren't thrilled at becoming the women's team leaders. Outdoor culture, though not as overtly macho like other cultures, still wrestled with the perception that women's apparel is the low end of the cool factor in the store. It was pretty lonely and a bit risky for a new manager."

Sean developed a strategy to ensure that this pilot would be a success. The purpose of designated staff specifically for the women's and men's apparel section was so they could build up a core competency. And because MEC is an organization where information can be disseminated very quickly, the stream of feedback started right away. Sean says, "This helped create a sense of a really quick win." But Sean understood that offering a separate women's section could also reveal fault lines, which, in his view, was a good thing. "Just having the section up and having the gaps exposed created the objective feedback that could pass throughout the organization. This supported the evolution toward gender intelligence."

The women's apparel team and team leader that Sean created became an advocate for all of women's needs. It was soon revealed that the information being collected on women's apparel was also relevant not just to apparel but the other product, like packs. The company began collecting information on everything associated with women consumers, especially as it pertained to fit. Sean explains: "This was one area where I knew we weren't all that stellar and it wasn't until we separated the apparel sections that it really took off—the negative feedback, that is. But this was all good. We already created a system and team on the ground to collect this information and feed it back to the organization."

There is something else that's germane in this evolution to a gender-intelligent retail ecosystem: MEC had very strong retail fundamentals to begin with—solid sales per square foot, good same-store sales, healthy revenue growth, well-developed staff training programs, human resource programs in place, a loyal and hard-working staff, and great products that provided excellent value. However, at the time, MEC's systems were not set up to mine data along the lines of gender. Sean had to rely on member and staff feedback to judge if the new store layout was actually working. Not surprisingly, feedback from the women members was extremely positive, but the biggest testament to its success was that Sean's layout is now the de facto standard for the rest of the stores.

Sean believes going organic is not for the timid. He says, "There's lots of emotions associated with gender. The issues have to be navigated and there is always confusion around motivations. The biggest barrier to change for retailers with respect to gender intelligence is not what you might think. It's not about the resources and less so about how the store looks or feels. The biggest barrier is the organizational culture and how the communication process is aligned. If it is not intuitive, it is not set up to be attuned to customer needs. This is where leadership comes into play."

GENDER-INTELLIGENT LEADERSHIP

Undoubtedly, MEC's biggest advantage in transitioning to a gender-intelligent ecosystem is that they are continually learning. Rooted within their DNA is a sensitivity to all MEC stakeholders—the environment and its members—and to the ideals of social awareness and responsibility. MEC did not become a green organization because women like to support environmentally friendly organizations. They were already green. Because they were green, they were also open, which is the winning formula to becoming organic.

The company has excellent corporate listening skills. Sean explains: "We are run by a consensus-based culture. This makes it easier for us to be sensitized to our regional markets. The culture is open to the information coming back from the stores as they gather feedback from the different trading areas that they serve."

What helped make the transition easier for MEC was its fairly flat leadership structure in the stores. The store managers are considered market experts in their trading areas and are encouraged through both formal and informal opportunities to provide feedback about things they are witnessing on the ground. The relationship between stores and the product managers who design and procure product is especially strong. Both the size of the country and MEC's structure have allowed this dynamic to thrive, with local managers able to represent the needs of their local markets. MEC, despite not being a franchised system, has such a strong value and mission of service that their local leaders feel a great deal of ownership over their stores.

Sean continues: "There are other business fundamentals that differentiate us from a lot of the other retail businesses out there."

- Executive compensation is under the norm for the industry and front-line salaries are ahead of the norm. As an example, the ratio between MEC's CEO and front-line compensation is 11 to 1; the average for similar businesses is 170 to 1.
- Open-door policy is practised at all levels of the organization and MEC's executive level is readily accessible. They always make themselves available to any staff for one-on-one meetings, both formally and informally.
- The average orientation training period for a new hire is 10 days (compared to an industry average for orientation of one to two days), and the organization commits significant resources to ongoing training as well.
- The employee turnover is lower than the industry average.
- MEC emphasizes values as much as it does technical knowledge and experience when hiring.

Clearly, people are a key critical component to what makes the organization tick. However, outdoor retail is a "destination shopping" experience. It is not a necessity such as grocery retail. What this means is that the experience has to be just that—an experience. Part of that is the physical surroundings.

GREEN BUILDINGS

As an outdoor retailer, it was important that the physical structures of the buildings reflected MEC's respect for the environment. Consequently, they were early adopters of green buildings. Most retailers are only now adding green building prototypes. MEC has been building green for over 10 years, and we mean everything—their retail buildings, head office, and distribution warehousing are all built to a green building standard. The buildings are built for easy accessibility from the outside; are near major transportation routes; and have a warm and welcoming exterior with lots of stone, wood, and windows for natural light.

The Inside

Inside MEC stores, the interior finishes are designed with the same natural aesthetic, relying as much as possible on natural lighting to illuminate the interior retail spaces. The Toronto store has a high cathedral ceiling with huge skylights that flood natural light into the interior.

Lighting

Sean has seen ancedotal evidence at MEC that natural light impacts women consumers' behaviour and store experience. He explains: "At MEC, we design most of our stores to maximize natural lighting . . . Although I have not seen statistical proof of its impact on direct sales, MEC stores overall have excellent sales per square foot, higher than the norm for our industry and higher than mall-based averages. Women appear to respond favourably to the amount of natural light that we've introduced into our buildings. The market overall has responded to the care that we take in building our stores and realizes that it is an authentic demonstration of our corporate values."

Merchandising Strategy

The store is laid out in a logical fashion based on what you would need to "get outside and play." Gear and the smaller items that are more frequently purchased are placed near the front, and clothing and apparel that generally take more time to purchase are placed farther inside the store.

When you walk into MEC, staff are immediately accessible, with member service desks placed right at the entrance. The service desks are staffed with the most experienced people and handle everything from complicated repair and warranty issues; the best place to go out and play; where to find good instruction or equipment rentals; or just help in finding items within the store.

The design of the store offers excellent sightlines so you can quickly determine where you want to go and get there easily. It's open with wide, uncluttered aisles, something women in the research reported was important. Those wide aisles also make it easier to navigate the store with strollers and kids. Because women frequently have children with them, the women's change rooms are larger to accommodate strollers. They are also designed for breastfeeding should women want privacy, but at MEC, women are welcomed to breastfeed wherever they feel comfortable. There is a family washroom that can accommodate a stroller and has change tables. There are also complimentary diapers.

MEC looks at everything to make the area work better for women, especially the so-called "small things," such as having more mirrors, lowering bar heights on the apparel racks, and changing the colour of the walls in the change rooms to provide better viewing conditions. While these details are rarely noticed from a customer's point of view, they make an impression at a subconscious level.

Safety and Parking

Sean became more interested in safety after he was asked to accompany a woman member to the underground parking lot. He implemented change such as overall improvements to lighting, security monitoring, and signage. MEC was looking at this not just as a parking lot but as part of women's experience in the store that needed to seriously improve.

MEC PUTS GENDER-INTELLIGENT PRODUCT DEVELOPMENT ON THE RADAR

Much of the change in the women's product line has been focused on the expansion of MEC women's apparel line. The other major change was the comprehensive review of MEC's fit and design patterns.

Sean says, "The design challenge is to constantly look at ways you can achieve both, having women in great-looking clothing that also offers the highest level of performance. This is something MEC strives for, never letting itself off the hook."

There has been continued growth, with women's apparel sales now almost matching the men's lines.

SALES TOOLS: MARKETING, ADVERTISING, AND THE WEB

Admittedly, MEC has been slow to evolve with traditional marketing. MEC hasn't made use of their vast database potential yet, though one can argue that their owner/member payouts at year's end amounts to a loyalty program as a member's ownership and, therefore, payouts are based on the total cumulative value of the person's MEC purchases.

The marketing department was officially created only four years ago. The majority of their budget is dedicated to producing their catalogues, though they now send out e-newsletters to members who request them. In terms of advertising, MEC does not do anything women-specific, nor should they. Their advertising shows a consciousness about women and they use strong visual images of women engaged in healthy, positive activity. Their advertising uses gentle humour, which very much appeals to women. Communications are always fun and educational. As Sean puts it, "We completely avoid the macho, sexualized images of women that you would find in climbing, cycling, or mountain biking magazines."

The company never had to advertise, building only on word of mouth. This organic growth was important to MEC, so it had to ensure that it was both creating communities and building relationships.

What studies have shown is that women's word of mouth is one of the most powerful drivers of business. When women find a service/business that meets their needs, they are extremely loyal. This has been Mountain Equipment Co-op's experience. It has grown its business entirely from word of mouth to its current position today—$250 million in annual sales. MEC is not a publicly traded company, so it does not get the coverage that a publicly traded company might. It does mail out, however, about $2 million annually in dividend cheques to its owners (i.e., members).

In reality, the company doesn't need conventional marketing because it isn't a conventional company. Indeed, it takes an organic approach, integrating its values into everything it does. Hence, the word-of-mouth marketing phenomena, known to be especially strong among women, is taking care of business.

In terms of company values, the company is diligent about making sure the inside of the organization matches whatever image is put forth out there. For example, ethical product sourcing is a corporate mandate. Forty-five percent of the company's products are Canadian, with the rest coming from Europe, the US, China, and Asia. Currently the majority of the clothing is private label, meaning that MEC contracts out its own designs to factories, which must meet strict approval standards. MEC uses its own supplier team evaluation program and third-party audit teams to screen sources. This information is publicly available in its accountability report, which is committed to reporting on all aspects of MEC's social and environmental impacts, warts and all.

Another of their aspirational goals is outdoor adventure and continued learning. One of the best examples of how this is developed internally is a long-range planning project that the organization engaged in called the Futures Project. MEC has committed to long-term planning with a ground-up development process that has engaged more than 800 staff and an equal number of members to develop long-range goals for the next 10–15 years. The three goals endorsed by the board and the membership are as follows:

1. Increase the participation in self-propelled wilderness-oriented recreation in Canada. One outcome of this goal will to ensure that more youth and children are active in the outdoors across the country.
2. Support the creation and stewardship of a comprehensive network of parks, wilderness, and outdoor recreation in Canada.
3. Change the marketplace toward environmental, social, and economic sustainability. MEC is committed to moving toward carbon neutrality and zero waste in its operations.

This is not a passive company. MEC is out there actively engaging in these issues and making a change. None of these initiatives is marketed or hyped, but the members feel it. It's one of the most trusted brands in the country. That is what we mean by intrinsic. This is not a marketing event, it's a company core competency. Values like these create an organization whose marketing costs are much lower than those of their industry peers, while member satisfaction and retention are higher. MEC continues to be the beacon for an organic standard of retailing today. Because they are continually evolving and have adopted a fluid, gender-intelligent process, chances are they'll stay top of the heap for a while against their larger competitors like the Forzani group (Coast Mountain, Sport Chek). MEC almost doubled in size in the last three years, adding five new stores across the country and more than 1 million new members. It has also earned international accolades for its transparency, its ethical sourcing policies, and its sustainable building and business practices.

The Web

MEC has a fully transactional website, but a key component of the site design is the community section. It isn't just about "selling stuff." It's also about learning, trading used gear, receiving bulletins and newsletters, and being informed about events and outdoor courses. The website is really just a reflection of how MEC creates their store environments, all of which offer many of the same components. The Internet has become as important a tool to build the MEC community as it is a channel to sell product.

TRAINING: CREATING GENDER-INTELLIGENT POINTS OF CONTACT

The company invests significantly in staff training. It is the company's view that this is the most efficient way to execute a corporate strategy and bring it to life. In the retail industry, the average salary-to-sale ratio is $12 to $100 of sales. At MEC, the salary-to-sale ratio is closer to $7 to $8. MEC doesn't encourage their sales staff to keep their chats short with customers. On the contrary, they are trained to provide the service that is required. But because they are so well trained, they can spend less time and are more cost efficient.

MEC's internal sales process is referred to as WAAC, which stands for Welcome, Assess, Address, and Complete. The staff aren't given a fixed time limit to spend with customers, which is particularly advantageous for women, who usually have a lot more questions. When staff are in training, they are not to sell anything but just listen to the customers' questions and respond. If anything, MEC sales staff can be accused of underselling; there are times the customers want to be told what they need and be sold on it.

IN SUMMARY

And although today MEC is a highly evolved organic retailer, Sean cautions that you have to pay attention to ensure that gender-neutral thinking doesn't creep in to day-to-day activities. Sean also had a clear understanding that an organic-standard retailer had to make a woman's life easier. His strategy, which started out as separate apparel sections, has evolved to include the many dynamics at play with women consumers. He explains:

> *We respect women's time.* MEC works hard to provide an information-rich environment, including the Internet. When women come into the store, the staff meet that level of knowledge provided on the website. Because of our mandate in education and information across all lines, the sales process is much faster and more efficient. Hence our relatively low staff cost-to-sale ratio and high customer satisfaction levels.
>
> *We meet women's level of service needs.* We've helped women get ready to climb Everest and we have helped them select a baby backpack carrier for their hiking trips. We are ready to service at both levels and everything in between.

We have created an enjoyable shopping environment. The family washroom, play area, and breastfeeding rooms all give the message "Women, you are welcome here."

We provide a uniform and complementary service experience across buying channels. Without leaving the comfort of their home, they are able to "walk across the floor" and talk to several technical experts all through one telephone call. The service centre staff are trained the same way that the store staff are, thus ensuring a uniform experience. Service centre store hours follow the store hours from Halifax to Vancouver. MEC customers can also order merchandise through the website.

Sean concludes, "Without the expansion of the women's membership base or product line, there would not have been an over 150 percent revenue growth in the last 10 years, with the majority coming from same-store sales. MEC remains one of the few examples that is delivering a product or service nationally through multiple channels in a gender-intelligent way."

MEC may define its success as an alignment of members' values with the delivery of product and services that meet their needs, but we have given it another name: gender intelligence.

ORGANIC STANDARD RETAILER
• Primarily relationship-oriented
• Truly engaged in a two-way dialogue with women
• Link product features to benefits, creates relevance
• Customer points of contact demonstrate excellent social skills

- Evidence of intuitive or learned gender intelligence
- Focused on relationship and retention versus one-time transaction
- Seeks to create a physical service environment focused on meeting women's needs
- Evidence that the service experience starts before women enter the front door
- Products and services are offered through a number of channels: bricks, clicks, and phone
- Service personnel have the authority to solve women's problems with minimal oversight
- Provides relevant information that helps women make an informed decision
- Diversity is intrinsic in all decisions
- Strong representation of women throughout the hierarchy of the organization who are enabled to make decisions
- Sophisticated use of language and images that reflect how women receive and process information
- Strong corporate social responsibility orientation (corporate soul)

CHAPTER ELEVEN

The Lay of the Land

When I have one foot in the grave, I will tell the whole truth about women. I shall tell it, jump into my coffin, pull the lid over me, and say, "Do what you like now."

—Leo Tolstoy, Writer

When Sean and I first began to write this book, Al Gore was just, well, Al Gore. Today he's a Nobel Peace Prize recipient for his work on the environment. Environmental movements like the 100-mile diet (eat local) were not at all well known. If you tried to explain this concept to someone as recently as three years ago, you'd be met with thought bubbles saying, "That's not only a little woo-woo, it's impractical and, frankly, obtuse." Today, it is becoming entrenched as a core ideology for those trying to achieve a more sustainable lifestyle. Its time has come. The dialogue has moved from "why" to "how."

When I first started talking to companies 15 years ago about the need for a conscious strategy to meet the needs of women, it was purely focused on "why." My average sales cycle was two to five years. Much to the delight of my bankers, this has changed. Sales cycles have tightened up dramatically because I no longer have to take the time to convince most companies on the "why." It's now moving toward "how."

The net of all of this is that companies need to take stock of their current ecosystem and move toward one that is women-centric and employs the organic principles of health, ecology, fairness, and care. Gender remains a stubborn barrier to a company's success, despite some significant societal changes. We leave you with this: When it comes to understanding women consumers, is your company's leadership operating as an integrated whole, or is the file folder or silo approach still in vogue? We've illustrated some impressive short- and long-term results that can come from simply integrating a wide-angle gender lens throughout your organization.

Thinking like an organic farmer really works. It's about leadership, being hands-on, getting down in the dirt, caring about details, and understanding the real issues that women face. Our hope is that this type of leadership will become more pervasive in the retail and service sector. Frankly, if we've done our job well, this book will become an interesting footnote in a historical context, but no longer relevant to the discourse on gender.

BECOMING A GENDER-INTELLIGENT RETAILER

- *Look at the business case.* Take a bold new look at your business and maximize the opportunity that women consumers represent for your company. You could be amazed.
- *Realize that change is hard work.* Help management realize the opportunity of focusing on women consumers. Be prepared for hard slogging, as the concept needs to be communicated and sold to colleagues and staff. Changing people's attitudes can be as much hard work as implementing the strategy itself.
- *Seek and establish leadership.* Gender-intelligent leadership can come equally from men and women within the organization.

- *Map your company and take stock of where you are right now on the gender-intelligence scale.* Identify the hurdles in organizational readiness, such as sunken investments in current structures, lack of leadership or sponsorship at the helm, unmotivated staff/culture, and traditional MAWG thinking. Innovation and a gender lens can come from disparate parts of the business, but the opportunity needs to be quantified.
- *Challenge the status quo.* Create a champion (the higher in the company's hierarchy, the better) and recruit supporters up and down the organization to reorient management on the goal of raising the bar for everybody by intelligently and authentically connecting with women.
- *Walk in women's shoes.* Make women the centre of the consumer experience by planning for their needs. Remember, if you meet women's needs, chances are good you'll exceed everyone else's.
- *Base your strategy on people.* Have staff in place to execute your strategies. This is not an approach that can be driven by technology.
- *Be aware that gender-neutral doesn't cut it.* Women and men are wired differently, which affects how they behave as consumers. The more a business understands this, the easier it will be to meet the needs of everyone.
- *Start thinking like a woman.* Adopt a holistic point of view in which *everything* is connected.
- *Eradicate women's PESTs.* Apply a gender lens to your entire customer experience process.
- *Pay attention to the details.* Product development, store design, sales tools, and training need to include the voices of

women. Train your managers and front-line employees so
they can develop their own internal gender lens. Women
are incredibly discerning consumers who pick up on virtually everything. No kidding.

- *Dump the "marketing-to-women" mindset.* It's not the marketing department's job to ensure that women's world views,
needs, and preferences are systematically taken into consideration throughout your whole organization and value
chain.

- *Identify the low-hanging fruit.* It's important to achieve quick
wins and gain support throughout the organization. A quick
win can often start with something as simple as adopting a
gender-inclusive language.

- *Don't fall into the pink-washing trap.* Gender intelligence
does not mean forgetting the needs of men, but is meant
to inform your thinking and creativity to consider both
genders' needs. Be ready to commit the necessary time,
money, and effort so that gender intelligence becomes a
core competency for your company and a sustainable differentiating factor for your brand.

- *Operationalize gender intelligence.* Gender intelligence needs
to be considered as important as other corporate objectives.
Have a plan for getting there. Set objectives and timelines
for meeting those objectives and try to achieve them. Hold
staff accountable to these objectives.

- *Take the journey.* Stop talking or keep talking, but start doing. Becoming gender intelligent is like staying competitive.
Success is in the journey and the realization that your work
is never done.

Index

Note: Page numbers in italics indicate material in charts and tables.